SOCIAL HOUSING

DEFINITIONS & DESIGN EXEMPLARS

Paul Karakusevic
Abigail Batchelor

RIBA Publishing

© RIBA Publishing, 2017

Reprinted 2017, 2018

Published by RIBA Publishing,
66 Portland Place
London W1B 1NT

ISBN 978-1-85946-626-1

The rights of Paul Karakusevic and Abigail Batchelor
to be identified as the Authors of this Work have
been asserted in accordance with the Copyright,
Designs and Patents Act 1988 sections 77 and 78.

British Library Cataloguing-in-Publication Data
A catalogue record for this book is available
from the British Library.

Commissioning Editor: Ginny Mills
Production/Project Manager: Michèle Woodger
Designed by Alexander Boxill
Typeset by Academic and Technical Typesetting
Printed by Pureprint Group

www.ribapublishing.com

Acknowledgements

This book would not have been possible without a number of individuals. Firstly, we would like to thank Thomas Feary and Edward Simpson, who undertook valuable research and played crucial roles in shaping and creating the book. Andrew Hopper for his drawing skills, as well as Kelly Tang and Violetta Boxill for steering the graphic identity, and Laura Cobb and Laura Egbi for their organisational rigour.

Secondly, we would like to thank the practices for contributing the information for the case study projects, including those who were not finally included in the publication, and the interviewees for giving their time and sharing their insights.

We also wish to thank the reviewers for their helpful suggestions, in particular Suzanne Prest, Tessa Baird and Andrea Klettner as well as Hugh Pearman, Ellis Woodman, Owen Hatherley and Oliver Wainwright.

About the authors

Paul Karakusevic, founding partner of Karakusevic Carson Architects, established the practice with the ambition of improving the design quality of social housing and public buildings in London. The focus for the practice is the delivery of successful neighbourhoods, mixed-tenure housing and civic buildings that reflect both their unique, local sense of place and the real needs of the communities involved.

Karakusevic Carson Architects has pioneered an approach to consultation and engagement that is meaningful and sensitive, creating a climate of trust and openness with clients and resident groups that enables projects to progress successfully with the highest quality outcomes.

In addition to his nationally and internationally recognised experience with the practice, Paul is a design advisor to the HCA/GLA, Urban Design London and Design Council/Cabe and lends his experience to audits, critiques, review and awards panels of major initiatives and projects across the UK.

Abigail Batchelor is an architect and urbanist who trained at the University of Sheffield and London School of Economics. She is a housing specialist with over 15 years' experience in the UK and the Netherlands and is an associate at Karakusevic Carson. A course leader on the housing and urbanism master's at the Architectural Association and a lecturer at London Metropolitan University, she has taught internationally and is a regular guest critic. She is particularly interested in the broader social and economic impacts of large-scale development and the meanings of place within a globalised market. Her research was presented at the Venice Biennale in 2014.

Editorial Contributor

Mike Althorpe is a researcher at Karakusevic Carson Architects and leads on learning at the practice. He studied fine art at Kingston University and completed an architectural history master's at the University of Westminster with a focus on London. Between 2007 and 2009 he was part of architectural thinktank Building Futures, and between 2011 and 2015 he was public programmes manager at the Royal Institute of British Architects. In 2012 he curated the institute's A Place to Call Home exhibition on mass housing and The Brits Who Built the Modern World in partnership with the BBC in 2014.

Introduction

1 Council housing

2 Renovation strategies

3 New processes among residents

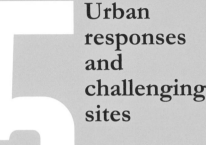

Introduction

Essay
Paul Karakusevic: A new era for social housing
Founding Partner of Karakusevic Carson Architects

After years of it being marginalised and viewed as an option of last resort, architects and designers are once again re-engaging with the 'social and public housing sectors.' Across Europe, a new generation of projects are playing a critical role in the reinvention of building and housing typologies, and piloting new delivery methods.

In the UK, record property prices and a considerable, well-documented housing shortage has brought about a crisis in affordability, partially a consequence of asset value being consistently prioritised over supply. Some have called it a "national emergency"[1] and it has led to a reversal in the trend of increasing levels of home ownership with a 2016 report by the Resolution Foundation finding that ownership in some parts of England was back to the same level as 1986.[2]

As the traditional UK private housing market fails to respond and struggles to offer any new ideas on how to increase the supply of housing, the initiative is now with a myriad of groups that includes local authorities, housing associations, co-operatives and consortia of motivated residents. Together, these formal and informal groups are redefining what we understand to be "social housing" and it is from the efforts of these re-energised groups that this book takes its cue. Karakusevic Carson Architects counts 13 local authorities across London as our clients. For several of these authorities, our projects represent their first public housing schemes for nearly four decades. This is hugely significant and it is this sea change in the ambition of the public sector to deliver high-quality housing that has spurred the creation of this publication.

The post-war years between 1945 and 1980 were a period of sustained large-scale investment in social housing, and estate construction all over Europe reached historically high levels of completions. During this time architects put into practice many utopian ideas and modernist experiments in model living. In doing so, they created some of the continent's most celebrated pieces of architecture. It is often overlooked that for many public bodies in the post-war years, offering "housing for all" was a sincere and diverse objective. It meant the creation of desirable, sophisticated dwellings and integrated accommodation for a range of income groups to help local economies and to provide housing for local residents, not just building the most basic for the poorest or those in most desperate need. Unfortunately, much post-war housing is now viewed in this way.

In pursuit of ever greater numbers, more expedient industrialised construction processes were adopted and design quality was undermined by poor construction; subsequently "council housing" in the 1970s developed a poor reputation. At the same time, the unintended consequences of comprehensive development and policies of decentralisation were beginning to be felt. Cities were losing their vitality, economic instability loomed, neighbourhoods were fractured and renewal programmes often broke up the very communities for whom the estates were intended. In many cases, those with the means moved away to seek new opportunities, leaving behind those tenants with least resource and most need just as industry started to enter a downturn.

The architectural profession's reputation was tarnished by its role in public housing projects – indeed for most of the 1980s they were scapegoated for their perceived failings, with the social geographer Alice Coleman's divisive and highly influential report, *Utopia on Trial*, delivering a fatal blow. Her Conservative government-sponsored "research" into problem estates published in 1985 helped shape official policy and popular discourse, and she unequivocally blamed architecture and design for their failure rather than exploring the roots and complexity of social problems and economic inequality. Hence it was no surprise that so many architects chose not to venture into an environment that appeared hostile to their ideas and suspicious of their expertise.

For a time it seemed that the architects had lost interest in housing. In the 1990s and 2000s, architectural debate was dominated by other building types, such as museums and galleries. There are good reasons for this of course. The UK needed new cultural infrastructure and these typologies allowed architects great scope for architectural freedom, but while this activity took place problems in social housing were stark. At the peak of all housing production in the UK in the late 1960s, the social sector could boast of

0.1   Council-led project billboard in the
      London Borough of Hackney

0.2   Dujardin Mews, new affordable
      housing in the London Borough of
      Enfield completed in 2017

0.3   Highworth Point, Trowbridge estate,
      Hackney, London, being demolished
      in 1987

completions per year of 175,550.[3] In 1996, the year before the Labour government took power, the number of homes built by councils and housing associations was just 34,860. However, in upbeat late-1990s Britain, any talk of crisis in the sector could be silenced by what was a buoyant private housing market, confident in its abilities and the unassailable narrative of universal ownership above all else. When in 2002–03 it was reported[4] that social housing numbers had plummeted even further to just 19,260, it did not seem to be significant.

In the years leading up to the 2008 economic crisis, the UK had the necessary financial liquidity, but lacked the will to invest adequately in social housing and as a result it lost ground. Under the last Labour government, the social mantle fell almost exclusively to housing associations who were able to complete some quality schemes, but did not themselves possess the resources to build at the scale required to tackle affordable housing shortages. In 2007–08, as the private sector put up 146,000 homes for private sale or ownership, housing associations in England managed just 24,100 completions,[5] their operations subject to the complexity of shifting government regulation, variable subsidies and caps. The clear lesson from these years is that we cannot expect one type of body to absorb the responsibility of delivering affordable housing. The future success of social housing requires multiple agencies and a diversity of suppliers acting in tandem.

Drawing together 24 case studies by 20 practices from eight European countries, this publication captures some of the best and most innovative examples of housing at a critical juncture for the sector. Produced in partnership with the RIBA, it looks at a range of carefully researched international models that together in the first decades of the 21st century, may be considered alternative forms of increasing social housing, offering possible solutions for the future and fresh thinking. The book brings together British and European examples in order to compare, contrast and learn from a range of distinct processes, public financing, procurement routes, building types and techniques. In this way, the publication aligns itself with pioneering housing publications of the early 20th century that showcased projects and emerging built habits from abroad in order

28 new Council homes for social renting, 39 for shared ownership and eight for private sale to help pay for them all in the absence of government funding

Range of 1-3 bedrooms

Redevelopment as estate uneconomical to refurbish

0.1

0.2

0.3

to re-energise debate, challenge established practice and raise standards.

This is the first book published by the RIBA on the subject of social housing and, in the 21st century, the definition of it exists in multiple forms. Across Europe there are many distinct methods for delivering housing and in many of the countries featured in this book the term "social" is rarely used at all. In the UK it is commonly (mis)understood as simply "council housing", in France it is "housing at moderate rent" (*habitation à loyer modéré*), in Denmark it is "common housing", in Germany "housing promotion", while in Austria it is "people's housing". Uniting all of these however, is the idea that there are and can be alternatives to a purely market-orientated system of provision and it is here, amidst the variety of alternative forms both new and old, that this book places itself. Within our definition of "social housing" we present here public projects led by local authorities, philanthropic schemes led by charities and co-operative or collective schemes led by residents and the people who will live in them.

Across Europe some form of strategic public oversight of housing supply has been maintained through a variety of means that includes direct building, subsidies, planning and rent control. The result is that while different nations have variable social housing trends ranging from low numbers in Germany to high in the Netherlands, for example, there is almost no talk of any comparable national crisis in supply. There are a myriad of reasons for this, from national economic conditions, regional differences in housing need and affordability of private housing. Even in the UK, housing needs between the south-east and north-west of England are incomparable.

Now after decades of being stripped of influence and land assets through land disposal, sell-offs and Right to Buy policies, local authorities are once again enabled, confident and taking the initiative as clients, with local oversight and a determination to get to grips with housing supply in their area. However, this public confidence should not be mistaken or misrepresented as a simplistic return to old-school state building. In the four-decade break in public activity, the culture and entire economic base of cities has shifted and housing

expectations have changed. Today local authorities are working hard and fast to develop in-house regeneration and development skills and to embrace a nuanced approach to delivery that takes on board the lessons of the post-war era and the recent past. This means financial modelling within strict credit limits, new procurement routes, mixing tenures and embracing typologies suited to local need and working to achieve the best possible standards of process and design.

Today cities all over Europe are grappling with the technical and social failings of older, mainly mono-tenure, estates and they have become areas for imaginative renovation strategies and joined-up urban planning, extensions and intensification. A new generation of practices is looking at public housing again in this way and from these projects we have selected the case studies.

Housing has a unique capacity to define urban form and the character of the city. In London, the city's historic networks of Georgian and Victorian terraces and squares are enjoyed by all – not just those who live in them – while in Paris its apartment blocks are an essential part of the urban experience and the life of its streets. Increasingly, through economic change and consumer choice, people are seeking out the opportunities of cities. The last decade of the 20th century saw London's population rise after decades of slow post-war decline.[6] This movement of people and the associated intensification of land use will be an ongoing trend in the coming decades and requires thoughtful and imaginative intervention.

When you work on an existing estate or neighbourhood scale, there is a unique opportunity to rethink the structure of an area, its connections, the quality of its buildings and how residents might better use and inhabit public space. New homes should be precursors of improved quality of life and this means providing housing that is integrated with the life of the town and city in which it is situated. In contrast to the UK, Europe has a long established "urban" tradition and its cities have largely retained their populations. In France and Germany it is not unusual to find high numbers of families and older people living at urban cores in compact residential flats rather than out in low-density suburbs.

Residents have a key role to play in the creation of successful and sustainable neighbourhoods. I take great pride in being able to say that my practice has a track record of forging positive relationships with the communities within which we work and it is a crucial part of the design process. Attitudes to new housing and development will not change by cynically withholding information or misrepresenting the intent of a project. Some key urban regeneration projects initiated in the late 1990s set an unfortunate precedent with regards to the status of residents, and nearly 20 years later a new generation is tackling understandable intransigence and suspicion. Ushering in new processes with residents means being upfront and for stakeholders of all kinds to be open to ideas to inform an agreed brief for both client and resident. It is also about empowerment and enabling those with an interest and means to do so to drive forward their own physical improvement projects should they wish, in partnership with local authorities and landlords.

This book's alternative narrative embraces those who want to create the homes they need by their own volition as groups and collectives. This is not contradictory to a social housing ethos, but rather a rediscovery of a grassroots form of social organisation, which when blended with the support and advocacy of a local authority or a housing association can be part of a positive mix in provision. The collective home model projects in this book have been selected to reflect this alternative route to delivery and because of their architectural merit.

Reforming and rebalancing housing provision is a long-term project. We are emerging from a 40-year economic and policy cycle, the consequences of which are all around us. It is likely to be another two to three decades before the new attitudes and approaches discussed in the book can become the normal way of doing things, but I am optimistic that it will happen and the projects in this book demonstrate that we have good reason to be. Our brave housing future will not be born out of siding with any single ideology or design ethos, but it will need to be strategic, and at the forefront of this are people and cities in all their nuance and variety. ■■■■■■

[1] Professor Christine Whitehead, Emeritus Professor of Housing Economics at London School of Economics. From Rising to the challenge: London's housing crisis report.
www.lse.ac.uk

[2] Analysis published by Resolution Foundation in 2016 found that home ownership in parts of UK was back to 58%, down from a peak of 71% in 2003.
www.resolutionfoundation.org

[3] Peak production for all housing in the UK was in 1968 with 352,540 dwellings completed. In 1969–70, UK local authorities combined completed 175,550 homes.
www.gov.uk

[4] Based on figures compiled by the UK government.
www.gov.uk

[5] Based on figures compiled by the UK government.
www.gov.uk

[6] By 1988 the population of London was 6.7 million, a decrease of around 22% since 1939. From GLA Intelligence, 2015 'Population Growth in London, 1939–2015.'
https://files.datapress.com

Interview
Neave Brown: Public housing in another time

Architect with the London Borough of Camden, 1960s and 1970s

When you were studying it was a revolutionary time for architecture. What were your own influences and drivers?

When I was a student in the early 1950s all types of building had to adhere to government programmes. The Abercrombie Plan, the notion of the greenbelt and the wave of new towns were all part of a wide urban renewal plan. There was a tremendous dispute between those who believed we should be starting everything from scratch and those who thought we had to repair and remake the city. When we were students, the dominant influence was from the modernist movement of Le Corbusier, the Bauhaus and Mies van der Rohe. Alvar Aalto was another influence at the time, who brought great poetry to the more functional notions of Modernism. In *Vers une architecture*, Le Corbusier talked of a home being a machine for living in but also that "architecture is a thing of art". When we started designing housing, we did "Corb-type" housing inspired by the *Ville radieuse*, which was building in geometric volumes in green spaces. But we felt it needed to evolve to relate to our own London context, culture and needs. All our teachers at the Architectural Association (AA) were modernists and together we were moving towards a critique of the movement. I don't want to come across as pretentious about it; it was simply the way we were thinking at the time. It wasn't so much ideology as a problem-solving attitude.

When I graduated, people like John Miller, David Gray, Alan Colquhoun, James Stirling and James Gowan were all working or had worked for Lyons Israel Ellis. It was a desirable place to work and I got an interview. They were very important architects so far as Brutalism was concerned, as they thought differently about Modernism and they also cared about more practical notions of building, such as layout, organisation and detail.

There seems to be a belief at the time that modern design could provide a way forward for all sorts of building typologies, including housing. Did the optimism of the time drive you?

It was an optimistic time, but it was also the reality. It was a widespread attitude developed from a high critique of 1930s Modernism. We weren't establishing ourselves intentionally as the pioneers of a modern society, it was simply the way things were. Having worked for Lyons Israel Ellis, I worked for two years in Middlesex County Council designing schools. All buildings we were building at that time were government sponsored and there was lots of innovation in layouts and detail. Almost nothing was done by the private sector. When the Labour government fell, there was a feeling that more should be provided by the private sector and this meant getting more involved in housing types, which were easily understood in terms of industrial building.

One of your earliest major projects was a co-operative residential development. How did that come about and how were you able to manage it successfully?

Everyone was feeling their way after the war. After designing schools I went into private practice, working on small projects, and I shared an office with a structural engineer called Tony Hunt and we worked together. As friends we got talking about how we didn't want to live in Victorian terraces anymore and decided to find our own site for our own project. We found a site on Winscombe Street in north London, and I thought it was wonderful. We formed a housing association over a weekend and decided it would be five houses. We then went to Camden Borough Council, invented a name for our housing society and asked for support to build housing. Inevitably it was to be carried out to government standards, pre-Parker Morris. All we had to do as a group of people was pull together enough money for the site. We believed Winscombe Street to be social housing.

How did you come to work at Camden Council and be under Sydney Cook?

Before I joined Camden, it was a bad time economically and several schemes had stopped. A friend of mine, Richard Gibson, went into the department just as Sydney Cook

0.4   Churchill Gardens estate, Pimlico,
      London (1963) was a landmark of the
      first wave of new post-war housing

0.5   Axonometric of Winscombe Street
      housing, Camden (1965)

0.6   Designed in 1966, Fleet Road housing
      was a precursor to Alexandra Road,
      Camden

started and he rang me to say that they were looking for people. I applied, having just finished Winscombe Street, and unbeknown to me lots of people from Camden went to see it. I then got the job at Camden but I couldn't immediately give up my private work, which included exhibitions for the Arts Council. That was a measure of the man Sydney Cook was, as he allowed me to work in the office while continuing my own projects. The first thing I did was an outline plan for an area in Camden Town. We had a big argument with the planners at that time as it was seen to be architects intervening in what was a planning issue. The planner responsible was from the London County Council (LCC) and was on the "hard" Modernist side of the LCC team, not the softer Scandinavian style.

At our Fleet Road project, our planners had initially suggested a scheme which had "strategic walkways" all around it and a high-rise rectangular block in the middle. I explained to Sydney Cook that this was a high-density scheme, but that I could achieve the same housing numbers with a low-rise building. He gave me the room to do it, which was an extraordinary thing to do because no one had worked like that before.

Your Fleet Road and Alexandra Road projects are hugely different in ambition and scale. How did the working environment at Camden change between these projects?

Between those two projects in the late 1960s attitudes changed and the idea of participation of people who are going to become tenants became very popular. It seemed to solve the ethical problem that was set by those who had problems with authorities "imposing" things. The logic followed that if you participated as a group of people you could generate something which had a "genuineness", which an imposed idea couldn't have. I don't share that idea.

The original chief of housing at Camden was a man named Llewellyn Rowley. He had no real architectural understanding and the idea of low-rise high-density was not in his line of thinking, but he accepted my position. He retired shortly afterwards in 1970 and housing was taken over by another individual who brought in a group of

0.4

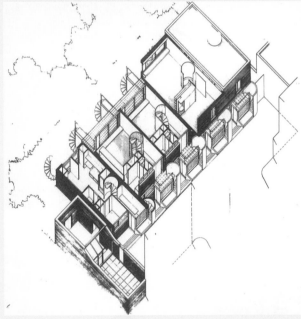

0.5

0.6

young council officers who were immersed in the notions of participation. Authority and approval had to be seen to come from the people and my outline designs for Alexandra Road caused an outrage.

Did Alexandra Road become an internal battle between the authority of the architect, your planners and the community?

When we were designing Alexandra Road we were not working with local groups in the way in which our housing team had begun to. Alexandra Road was a totally cleared site. The thing about participation was that it had to involve local people, otherwise they had no way of having legitimate rights over anyone else. With the planning brief we had and the freedom we had to design, we had clear authority for the design we did. We could then take it to the politicians. If the planning officer had objected to the development then the politicians would have been very concerned about it.

When in 1969 Alexandra Road went to committee, the new housing group was totally antipathetic to the idea of the authority of the architect and wanted things to expressed by the people. I had designed it as I thought the situation needed it, but the planning department was horrified. Across the UK there was a general attitude that assumed the unpopularity of local authority-designed housing. This was not the same thing as we were doing in Camden.

After Alexandra Road was accepted, it was disliked by the planning department who had conducted surveys on what people wanted. One particular question was: "Where would you like your kitchen to be?" and the most popular answer was: "next to the front door." Now the kitchens at Alexandra Road were on the upstairs level in the furthest corner because that made an infinitely more subtle, flexible and adaptable plan. Fortunately, when I was working we had the opportunity from Sydney Cook to be more authoritative. Some of those issues were so extreme that we had a terrible time getting housing to agree to committee approval and the planners wouldn't approve it. It was convention that you did not take a scheme to committee without the approval of both the housing department and the planners.

Sydney Cook was able to back my scheme and take it to committee without the authority of the planners. That was an unprecedented thing at that time.

How much did external political change threaten the project?

After Alexandra Road was committed, there was a change in government, and soon after a meeting was called between Sydney Cook and people from housing and planning to discuss a new strategy. Sydney Cook allowed me to go in his place and it included politicians, councillors, contractors and building system technicians. They put forward a Conservative programme which was based on industrialisation, sanitisation, prefabrication using pre-cast concrete, bulk buying of products, preferred dimensions and metrication, which they were trying to impose on us. Once you accept all that, there isn't much you can do apart from the housing that big industry wants to do. None of this had anything to do with the type of housing people wanted to live in, the only driver was the number of housing to be delivered and it was a total rejection of the attitude set up after the second world war by the Labour party. They supported it because they believed they could produce more units this way. I pointed out that we have a set-back building on a curve, which you could not possibly do with preferred dimensions and mass production.

As architects today we are under pressure to achieve numbers and density because there is a huge housing need, as there was when you were working. Did you also feel that pressure?

In the years after the second world war, the Labour party set out a programme through the (LCC) on what housing should be. The standards were high and when it came to the production of housing it usually came in two forms: one as often large Corbusian slab blocks and one as mixed development based on the English interpretation of Scandinavian housing. What is often overlooked is that Nye [Aneurin] Bevan refused to do more housing

0.7 View of housing and outdoor space
    use at Alexandra Road, Camden

0.8 Alexandra Road housing, Camden,
    pictured soon after completion

0.7

0.8

than he thought appropriate. The Labour government was opposed to working purely to numbers for fear of standards suffering. It was about quality of housing for society in the long term, not just immediate need. After the war the targets per year were around 200,000 units, but this changed depending on the government at that time. The housing standards also changed depending on the government. As soon as the Conservative government came in under Churchill in 1951, it wanted to raise the numbers of houses completed and in order to do that it wanted to use the building industry.

In replanning the cities after the war, the government carried out an assessment of appropriate densities. It was quickly discovered that people gravitated to the areas where they could find work, generally in the south, which meant that the government's figures in many places were quickly obsolete. There were a lot of areas where housing was being built without the appropriate demand but the attitudes towards density were deep-rooted. And unfortunately this led to some bigger projects in the north being unpopular and quickly failing.

How did the question to address the housing challenge sit within a strategic vision for the city? Did they work well together?

There are of course situations where uses don't mix and cases where they do mix. Where they do mix they need to be part of the proposition and not a problem to be solved later. The system now seems set up as a series of bits rather than a set of joined-up social ideas. The post-war London Plan, for example, meant that every inch of the city was planned right up to roads, density, transport and other uses. When you did a housing scheme, it had to follow the requirements of the plan. Every local authority had to accept these overarching planning rules as part of a joined-up city plan.

Many clients are often afraid of variables and taking risks. Was it always an advantage having the state and colleagues as your client?

It was much easier in my time. Today you're working with clients who are being advised by contractors, who are dealing with employer's agents, who are dealing with you, and you have a situation of competing priorities and objectives. On Alexandra Road you had housing, school, community centre and a public park, all of which were part of the public system. It was complicated but it was in an easier sequence of authority than nowadays. We had a clearer position of authority than generally seems to exist now. I could insist on things and get them built and designed with confidence.

How did your experience of working in the Netherlands differ from that in the UK?

I worked on a scheme in The Hague first and then Eindhoven. At Eindhoven there was a mix of government-sponsored social housing set at two levels and private

investment for luxury towers. It was a complex client. In the UK capital sums were set without a commitment to, or an understanding of, the lifespan of a building. Local authorities would often find themselves building buildings with large construction budgets but with no budget commitment for future maintenance regimes. In the Netherlands these calculations are set out from the start so that the whole life of the building is part of the finance proposition. Based on the premise that buildings get more valuable as they get older, a requirement is put in place for an equity base or covenant for future developments. When you are working on a building you are not just doing it and then walking away from it, you are doing something for the life of the building. When you do a private building for a private client, he or she probably has an idea for maintenance, whereas public authorities had no such planning in place. Without a commitment for maintenance and management we will continue to face the same series of problems we saw in the later post-war years.

Do you think that relative open-mindedness helped when, for instance, you had pursued things in terms of material and detail which perhaps wouldn't go with a traditional idea of homeliness?

You've raised an important issue. The detailed design is separate from the massive ideological issues which you bring into overall design. I had the freedom to think the way I wanted to think and there wasn't anything like the complexity that exists now. It was an idea of an egalitarian society that was developing from the inter-war years and highly ambitious social notions about a change from a capitalist society using design after the war and rethinking the models from before the war. It wasn't a new world but an applying of new ideas into an existing world. That dialogue between those sets of ideas was vital to the way we thought.

You describe the design process as iterative and that it changed along the way. Did you have a firm set of ideas about the house and what it should or shouldn't have?

Of course. You were trying to satisfy a cloudy notion of what you thought you wanted to do but didn't exist yet. It became clearer and clearer as you worked on it. On Alexandra Road for example it didn't take me long to realise that I wanted to do two strips of housing with a walkway down the middle. Fleet Road was far more complicated, however, to get right.

Did Alexandra Road ever reach a low point, as can be seen in the history of Park Hill in Sheffield for example?

The people who wanted to move in to Alexandra Road moved in and loved it. It now has a good interrelationship between those who exercised their Right to Buy and an existing community, and they are very active socially. Isn't that a good thing? We need to change the current system. We now have a segregated London and people who need to work in London have to live further out. We are losing our mixed population and that has to be at the forefront of everyone's minds.

There is a conversation at the moment that many 1960s estates should be retained as a piece of post-war London history. What do you think should be the approach to estates which aren't as successful as others?

Of course it is down to each individual site. There are some 1960s estates which should undoubtedly be pulled down. On the other hand, it is difficult to do that when you still have such a great housing need. You are faced with a difficult decision when what you are doing might exacerbate the problem rather than solve it. In our time it was a relatively easy situation. We could fight over a certain set of values.

One of the things that architecture has to do is resolve a situation of complex values which might be in conflict. If you're building a large building, all sorts of people are going to be involved and you have to find a hierarchy that you can work with. You can't respond to each and every individual person's values.

You have to come up with a proposition and see it through.

Looking back, what was it that set Camden apart from other local authorities? How was Camden able to achieve what it did?

Sydney Cook was exceptional. He took on board that things needed to be done in a different way and most of all he listened. He listened to people like Peter Tabori, Gordon Benson, Alan Forsyth and myself. He was eager to listen to new ideas. He didn't come in with precise social ideas on housing and rebuilding, but he understood that a new approach was needed to rebuild Camden.

We didn't talk much, however, to other local authorities in London. There wasn't a sense of competition between us, just a sheer determination to get things done at a local level. It was day-to-day involvement and the muscles you flexed were simply the ones you needed to flex. It's easy to sound that one was more pioneering than one was. Camden was only formed as a borough in 1964 by combining Hampstead, Holborn and St Pancras. This was around the same time as the introduction of the Parker Morris standards. For instance, it was much more specific to budget when related to density. It was more complicated in terms of car provision, roads and transport and all sorts of different factors were incorporated to assess budgets and efficiency of each scheme. It was immensely complex, but within the regulations there was a flexibility that allowed for experimentation and new types of housing for the future city. ■■■■

In the 1960s and 1970s, Neave Brown worked as an architect for the London Borough of Camden, widely regarded as one of the most progressive local authority architectural departments in the country and headed by Sydney Cook. In 2014 he became the first architect to have all of his UK work listed. His projects and experiences in social housing recall an era where local authorities were able to innovate and build in a manner unknown today.

Interview
Finn Williams: A time to innovate
Regeneration Manager, Greater London Assembly (GLA)

The definition of social housing is far removed from its original meaning and now includes a wide variety of tenure types. What is your understanding of social housing today?

Social housing has a long semantic history dating all the way back to philanthropic housing, to council housing, and now market discount or starter homes. This changing terminology shifts in political attitudes with housing seen as something earned, to being a universal right and back again. What we've seen since we stopped building council housing in the 1980s is a disconnect between the market and the reality of what people can afford. That now goes beyond social rent and council housing to people in the Private Rental Sector. It's something we explored in Home Economics[7] where we commissioned essays on the housing crisis in the form of 11 charts. Each chart shows the polarisation between those who are wealthy enough to own – who only get wealthier – and those who can only afford to rent. It demonstrates that it is more expensive to be poor than rich. For me, the definition of social housing should be linked to the reality of getting a pay cheque or subsidy from the state – as a percentage of income, rather than market discount.

Hackney Council's Colville Estate project is one example of effective cross-subsidisation to provide affordable housing. However, Barking Council does not have that luxury, given that land values are not as high in the outer boroughs. Do you see cross-subsidy as a long-term housing solution?

In the context of reductions in government grant, combined with the cap on housing revenue account borrowing (HRA), councils who want to build social housing are currently left without much choice, but this isn't just an issue for housing. In other areas we're seeing that public investment once funded through top-down taxation and redistribution now has to be derived from devolved forms of cross-subsidy. Rather than fund public infrastructure on a national basis, we now fund it on a local plot-by-plot basis, often through section 106 agreements or community infrastructure levy. The equation behind this cross-subsidy is increasingly visible on London's skyline, as we build higher in order to fund more things. It's a pragmatic short-term response to the current political climate; however, in the end that's probably not a sustainable way of building a city.

How can local authorities use their own land holdings to increase home numbers and diversify supply?

Until recently, the default strategy for delivering numbers of homes on public sector land was to dispose of it through freehold sales to the private sector. This raises capital in the short term, but it doesn't leave public authorities with much control over delivery. It also involves land being parcelled up and tendered to larger housebuilders, as a result of perceived inefficiency of public sector procurement. It's the path of least resistance but it also carries greater risks in terms of quality and delivery, which tends to happen in fits and starts.

There's a growing realisation that we can't become overreliant on a small number of large housebuilders shouldering so much of the burden of housing delivery in the UK. They're delivering, but still not at the scale we need. The public sector has a role to broaden the base of who builds housing and not just fuel the same machine. So it's exciting to see local authorities now starting to keep hold of their land and build homes themselves. Holding onto land to generate revenue income rather than disposing of it for capital receipts looks like a more sustainable way of maintaining public services over the longer term.

In London, there's a real opportunity to work at the opposite end of the spectrum from the major housebuilders and start to harness the ability of the crowd to deliver small schemes, at scale. If you look at public land on the London Land Commission register, which covers GLA, Transport for London, Network Rail, the NHS and borough ownership, there is huge potential for infill development. The opportunities are there, but in the context of a relative lack of in-house resources and expertise, there's a perception that it isn't efficient for the public sector to trawl through their portfolios and draw red lines round small pockets or corners of land.

0.9   Croydon's distinctive townscape
taken from the top of its many
multi-storey car parks during London
Open House

0.9

One of the things I have recently been involved in is a pilot programme to crowdfund civic projects, which shows that there is a different way. Where the GLA might traditionally have invested £1.3m into a single scheme, we have trialled investing the same amount in pledges of up to £20,000 towards around 80 community-led projects on the basis that they crowdfund the rest. Typically, the communities crowdfund more than double what the GLA puts in, and of course the real benefit isn't just building the projects, but that the programme is building the capacity of community groups. Also, by taking a portfolio approach it means you can afford to be more experimental as you are spreading your investment.

Applying that model to housing as part of a mixed portfolio approach unlocks a whole new set of opportunities for the smaller end of the sector. That would really help small and medium enterprise (SME) developers as well as self-builders, co-housing groups and Community Land Trusts (CLT).

We often hear from developers that more units or more affordable homes within a scheme are just "not financially viable". Is there a need for more regulated and standardised viability assessments in order that everyone can understand them and ensure greater contributions for low-cost housing?

Planners, politicians and the public are more and more aware of the formative role of viability in the current planning system – and councils are becoming more sophisticated about how they're used, or abused. It's certainly recognised at a London and national government level that the inconsistency and lack of transparency of assessments needs to be addressed with clearer guidance. But of course that's only part of the equation because you can write guidance, but in the end the policy is only as good as the officers on the ground who are translating it at local authority level. Good officers can work around insufficient policies, but good policies don't necessarily work around insufficient officers.

Viability is just one example of a system where the odds are stacked against the public sector as a result of a lack of resources. What we need is for working in the public sector to be seen as a privilege again, as opposed to a last resort. There's a whole generation of talented planners, architects, engineers, even chartered surveyors, who would like to work for the public good but wouldn't consider applying for a job in a council.

When I moved from private practice to Croydon Council, it was fairly unusual amongst my peers. If I'd stayed in the private sector I probably would have ended up setting up my own practice and designing residential extensions for friends of my parents. But working in Croydon's placemaking team was a bit like having our own small office, with a guaranteed flow of work, the freedom to make decisions for the public good rather than private profit, and the luxury of really getting to know a place and its people – rather than being parachuted in and out of places on a contract.

In 1976, 49% of architects worked in the public sector. Today, the percentage in London is only 0.13%.[8] There's been a paradigm shift in what we see the public sector as representing, particularly at a local government level. In the 1970s, councils were building the places that we lived in, learned in and our public spaces. They were where you went to work if you wanted to get things done. But with council housing grinding to a halt and an increasing reliance on the private sector to provide infrastructure, the function of "doing" in local authorities was more or less lost. It's starting to come back through the pioneering boroughs that are beginning to build again, and potentially through new initiatives like Homes for Londoners. But rebuilding that capacity is a bit like exercising muscles that haven't been used for years – it won't be easy.

One of the common clichés of development is that if we rolled back planning we could set housing free and solve the crisis. Is there any truth in this?

Not really. Politicians and policymakers need to see planning as part of the solution to delivering housing rather than part of the problem. If you look at a recent survey carried out by Knight Frank,[9] where they asked developers: "What is the single thing government could do to boost housing numbers?" the top answer was not give us free land or scrap regulations, but: "just resource planning departments properly."

The model behind my Public Service proposal[10] is to set up an independent social enterprise that gives councils access to a pool of the most talented and committed place-making practitioners at cost-price, cross-subsidised by the private sector. The more enlightened commercial developers, housebuilders, housing associations, and even consultants, recognise that good development relies on good planning and they are all keen to contribute. In some ways they already do this on a case-by-case basis through planning performance agreements and pre-application fees, but Public Service offers a more strategic and constructive route for them to help councils build long-term capacity in a way that is also far less open to exploitation. While councils would pay for the core salaries, private sector support will cover programme-wide costs, including recruitment, administration and training, making it far more affordable for councils than employing private agency staff. It's basically a not-for-profit version of an employment agency, an agency with real agency.

Do you think there is room for new methods of housing provision to enter the market, for example in custom or self-build developments?

There is definitely room and need for new models of delivery and – no one model will fix the housing

shortage. At the moment, the dominant model is volume housebuilding. We need to supplement this with more council-led housebuilding, and by using public land more intelligently to create opportunities for builders at the smaller end of the sector. We forget that the greatest proportion of new homes in London are delivered on sites below 0.25 hectares (0.62 acres), which fall below the radar of the Strategic Housing Land Availability Assessment and outside the core scope of local plans. Aside from deregulation and permitted development, planners' tools are generally too cumbersome to engage constructively in these kinds of conversions, extensions and infill schemes. But given how vital this scale of development is to London's housing supply, there have to be smarter ways of expanding delivery. We've talked about how we can build a platform to crowdsource small public sector sites on a leasehold basis. The public sector could also help SME developers or co-housing groups with promotion of site opportunities, preparation or coordinating and improving access to finance.

There's a chance that working with smaller sites might also help defuse some of the concerns about council-led housebuilding, which aren't just political, but also cultural. The last time the public sector built housing at scale in London was in the 1970s, and it tended to be on huge sites with single-tenure estates designed at a single stroke. They were often bold and experimental schemes, but if they failed, it was on a huge scale. Parcelling up rather than packaging up public land would have the advantage of delivering more mixed tenures, varied architecture and diverse places, and it would allow experimentation.

How could we make small sites work better for affordable housing?

A different approach to procuring development partners for public sector land could help. With smaller sites, you should be able to fix the price upfront. So instead of bidders looking to drive down the public contributions or quality of a scheme in order to bid highest, they have to demonstrate how much extra affordability or social value they can create and compete on that basis. The difference between

0.10 Skills in action at Croydon College
     open day

0.11 Putt Putt (2013): conceived to
     encourage alternative activity
     in Croydon

0.10

the short- and long-term values of this approach can be balanced across a portfolio of sites in order that the more profitable schemes can cross-subsidise others with more affordable housing.

How can the GLA help the boroughs develop their own development platforms in future?

That's a really interesting question. It's exciting to see how different boroughs are innovating, but you obviously want to avoid each local authority reinventing the wheel in isolation and creating a situation where quality differs across the city. There are already discussions within the GLA about a centralised viability team that could be made available to boroughs. And I've already mentioned my Public Service initiative, which could help boroughs to quickly build development teams – not just architects and urban designers but also chartered surveyors, housing specialists and so

0.11

on. I imagine it could also be useful to have a dedicated centralised team dealing with compulsory purchase orders. The challenge is how the GLA can support boroughs in a way that helps to build their long-term capacity, rather than superseding them.

Some developers view the Mayor's demands on housing standards as a barrier to development. What's your view on that?

The Mayor's London Housing Design Guide has been one of the most extraordinary achievements of the GLA. But it's interesting to see how the standards are now being questioned by new models of co-living, and a new generation of "disruptive" developers. These new typologies do ask some fundamental questions, not just about the standards themselves, but really about how we live today. This was looked at in Home Economics. The way we live is changing rapidly. It's a reflection of the increasing impossibility of home ownership, the growing number of people living month to month on insecure tenures, changing household structures, new technologies, and more generally mass mobility across different social groups. At the scale of the neighbourhood it's creating more fluid communities. But it's also dissolving our traditional ideas of the way we lay out our homes. For example, last year the bed overtook the sofa as the most used piece of furniture in the home. We now spend more time looking at screens than sleeping and just an average of 20 minutes every day cooking and washing up. It could be time to review the guide, not necessarily to make units smaller or cheaper, but simply to be more flexible to the way that domestic life is changing.

How do you think we might better align the demand for working and making spaces with that for housing?

Well, firstly the two-dimensionality of current planning tools doesn't help. We tend to look at a land use in plan, but could get better at thinking about how uses could be combined three-dimensionally. Another part of the story is the way development is financed. The majority of housing in the UK is based on getting a quick return on capital investment where a volume housebuilder finds a site, builds their housing, and sells off the units as quickly as possible so that they can move on to the next one. Longer-term ways of adding value to a place through other uses like workspace or maker-space are of less interest to that investment model. Investors tend to look for more certainty and less risk, meaning more "safe" commercial uses like urban supermarkets. Where a more mixed set of uses has been allowed to take hold is where there has been a long-term ownership and stewardship of land, for example in the great estates. Good landlords curate the mix, where the less profitable uses contribute to the quality of a place and are cross-subsidised by the more valuable uses. This patient model of investment doesn't fit with the short-term horizons of current volume housebuilders; it's an approach that's being adopted by more and more commercial developers, as well as larger housing associations and council-led housing programmes.

Do you think it might be possible to enable councils to have more flexibility in terms of provision of ground floor uses?

Culturally, there are still barriers to what kind of workspace people can imagine being integrated with housing. But, technically, there's no doubt that it's now possible to build very different kinds of workspace within housing-led schemes and the most appropriate area for this is the ground floor. At a London-wide level, the GLA is piloting new forms of open workspace provision in new geographies and different sectors, for example the building sector or the catering trade. Workspace doesn't necessarily have to mean people who work on laptops. The nature of making is also changing – digital manufacturing means it's not always noisy and smelly anymore. But making space that genuinely works for a mix of ground-floor uses does rely on a few simple, practical conditions, such as taller floor-to-ceiling heights and good service access.

How much do you think renovation and reuse of stock could play a role in addressing housing shortages? Is there more we could do in the UK to promote this?

I think using what we've already got should be our starting point before we even talk about new completions. In NOVUS' paper on council housing[11] we worked out that for every one new home completed in London there are 130 existing homes, 30 of which are underoccupied. In any year we are adding less than 1% of housing stock in London. In fact, the net increase in London's housing is not all down to increasing construction; it's also due to decreasing demolition and more conversions. At the current rate it will take 700 years to replace London's housing stock entirely. So a small uplift in how efficiently we use the 99% of existing buildings is going to make a much bigger difference to housing supply than concentrating on improving the efficiency of the 1% of new builds.

From the bedroom tax to schemes for moving out empty nesters, I think policy attempts so far on this front have been heavy-handed. Where someone chooses to live and how they use their space are personal things that traditional planning tools are just far too clumsy to influence. However, if you start thinking about occupancy over time, then there might be other ways of harnessing the dynamics of the sharing economy to incentivise people to use existing space more efficiently.

In fact, a lot of the factors that make the biggest difference to housing supply in London today fall outside the formal controls of planning policy – whether it's density of occupation, the way development is financed, or the many minor projects like conversions that make up the vast majority of delivery. We're putting a huge amount of effort and expectation into this small percentage of brand new homes, when we could be using new design approaches to find more intelligent ways of unlocking existing capacity.

How do you think we can make it easier for people to take the initiative to build their own houses or collaborate with others to do it themselves?

When you're competing on sites with a market that is looking for short-term returns rather than creating social value, competition for land is very difficult. There needs to be intervention from the public sector to level the playing field where public land is involved, but in a time of squeezed resources, councils are also under pressure to capture as much value from their land as possible. Different local authorities are taking different approaches, and who is to say it's wrong to sell off the highest value land to the highest bidder to fund vital social services, for instance? But there needs to be recognition that offering land to resident-led groups is not necessarily worse "value" than selling it to the highest bidder – it's just a different kind of value. And it's only by taking this longer-term and wider view of value that we're going to be able to build truly social housing. ▬

Architect-turned-planner Finn Williams has worked for the Office for Metropolitan Architecture, Croydon Council and the GLA, where he is regeneration area manager for north-west London. He is founder of Common Office and the planning thinktank NOVUS.

[7] Home Economics, exhibition of the British Pavilion at the 2016 Venice Architecture Biennale, explored how domestic space is used.

[8] '49% Architects in public sector 1976 and 0.9% nationally (and 0.13% in London).' ARB Register accessed December 2016. www.arb.org.uk/

[9] 74% agreed. Featured in Housebuilding Report 2016, by Knight Frank. May 2016. http://content.knightfrank.com

[10] An initiative launched in 2015 to embed talented young professionals within public authorities in order to develop the public sector's capacity for proactive planning. www.farrellreview.co.uk

[11] NOVUS is a group of young public-sector planners under 40. Their paper was published in July 2015. www.planningofficers.org.uk

1.1
Colville Estate, UK
Karakusevic Carson Architects

1.2
Agar Grove, UK
Hawkins\Brown + Mae

1.3
Silchester Estate, UK
Haworth Tompkins

1.4
Goldsmith Street, UK
Mikhail Riches

Council
housing

Introduction

Since the Industrial Revolution there has been a desperate need for housing in our cities and people who have been prepared to address the problem in different ways. In the 19th century it was the industrial philanthropists whose patronage first brought about affordable housing. Responding to the dire conditions of the poor, these charitable – but primarily commercial – men of enterprise formed the basis of social provision both in the UK and in Europe in the form of housing associations and co-operatives. They were the pioneers, not only in championing the cause of the poor and identifying an acute market failure, but also in putting architects to work in the development of so-called "model dwellings", and in doing so delivering homes to a previously unseen standard.

Spurred to act by campaigners and voters, in the 20th century municipal authorities and the state recognised that improved housing and planned development could play a role in creating a more egalitarian society. Housing was a moral and political crusade and cross-party consensus ensured a mid-century "golden era", where the public sector pursued construction with zeal, bringing to life the radical ideas of a new generation of designers and urban reformers.

Since the 1980s the retreat of the state, a ban on local authorities building, rising land values, slashes in subsidies and a focus on market-led provision and private home ownership has contributed to our current crisis and low housing completions. Once again, not enough homes are being built, with those that are, priced well beyond the means of lower- and middle-income groups, especially in major cities.

Affordable housing need in many parts of the UK is chronic and no longer confined to the poorest in our society. A 2015 English housing survey[1] found that, on average, tenants in the private rental sector in England paid half their monthly income on rent. In London the figure was even higher at two-thirds of the average take-home salary. In recent years, extortionate private rents have pushed up housing benefit bills, as councils dealing with extreme local shortages are forced to pay private landlords to accommodate their own social tenants and people on the waiting list. However, local authorities now have the capacity and support to start doing things differently.

In 2006, in the last throes of the Labour government, the rules on local authority borrowing, funding mechanisms and procurement were changed.[2] The impact of this little-reported act is now being felt as the public sector begins to build again. In 2002–03,[3] all UK local authorities combined built just 180 dwellings. By 2010–11, this figure had jumped to 3,130. The shift is substantial and set to grow in the coming years.

This chapter focuses on projects by local authorities building new housing and tackling the crisis for themselves. Its UK focus has been chosen because this is something of a quiet British revolution and a culture change unmatched by other European nations, whose policies have been much more consistent. The projects are "social" in terms of the state providing housing at reduced rents on public land, but are typically cross-funded through the sale of private homes and require neighbourhoods to be built at higher densities than previously. Hence they are not without controversy.

Despite sell-offs of land and property, and considerable pressure for them to release and sell more, local authorities remain some of the largest landowners in the UK, with expansive estates often in prime locations. Working in collaboration with housing associations, the projects demonstrate how local authorities as enlightened clients are thinking imaginatively about the future of their holdings. Addressing the failings of challenging estates, they are responding at a brave and ambitious urban scale, often with great sensitivity in order to secure the longevity of communities and create diverse and liveable pieces of city. Recurring themes in these projects include increased density, diversified tenure types, improved connectivity to adjacent areas and better functioning street frontages and public realm. ▪▪▪▪▪

[1] English Housing Survey Headline Report 2013–14 published by The DCLG.

[2] Reform started by Labour was carried forward by the Coalition government in 2010 and new self-financing system for local authorities enshrined as part of the Localism Act. Subsequent changes and reviews from 2012 have led to gradual increases in borrowing powers. www.gov.uk

[3] Based on figures compiled by the UK government www.gov.uk

1.0.1

Peabody flats, Westminster, London
by Henry Darbishire, 1870

Spurred into action by the horrific slums of London, Peabody was established by the American philanthropist and social reformer, George Peabody (1795-1869). Catering for the respectable poor, Peabody's first scheme appeared in 1864 and later estates followed a standard layout consisting of simple rectilinear blocks in stock brick grouped around small squares with flats sharing lavatories and sculleries. Solid and robust, these buildings established new standards but were often criticised for their architectural formality.

1.0.2

Victoria Square dwellings, Manchester,
by Henry Spalding, 1894

This was Manchester's first municipal housing intervention in a notorious industrial slum close to the city centre. Taking a robust and confidently urban character, Victoria Square is comprised of 237 double and 48 single tenements, and built to accommodate 825 people arranged around a large quadrangle occupying an entire city block. Communal laundry facilities and drying rooms were provided in each of the corner towers, along with main stairs to the continuous decks.

1.0.3

Boundary Estate, Shoreditch, London, by the LCC
architect's department under Owen Fleming, 1890-1900

Credited as the world's first council estate, the Boundary Estate was a pioneering development by a new and ambitious municipal authority. With its bold Arts and Crafts aesthetic, it introduced architectural distinction to social housing and was hugely influential. One thousand and sixty-nine dwellings are provided over 23 blocks set on broad, tree-lined streets arranged in a radial plan with amenity space, shops and workshops provided alongside the retention of schools and a church.

1.0.4

Golden Lane Estate, City of London,
by Chamberlin Powell & Bon, 1952-57

One of the first wave of post-war local authority housing schemes, the Golden Lane Estate became a landmark for its bold modernist design and open planning, creating amenity, visual variety and a range of public and private spaces. Created by a young team of architects, the estate was the result of a high-profile competition and reinvented an area devastated by wartime bombing. Mainly consisting of one- and two-bedroom dwellings, the housing was originally intended for single people and couples.

Interview
Karen Barke

Head of Estate Regeneration, London Borough of Hackney

What is the main barrier to housing supply?

It's clear that as a country, and especially as a city, we need to build thousands more new homes. Local authorities and housing associations want to build these homes, but are being hamstrung by government policy, which unnecessarily restricts our ability to deliver them in the numbers we want to.

The biggest barrier for local authorities is the artificially low housing revenue account (HRA) borrowing cap. Without being able to borrow effectively against future income, councils simply cannot access the funding needed to deliver the number of new homes we need. The government must lift this cap so that councils can demonstrate a commitment to building new housing.

The arbitrary restrictions on spending Right to Buy receipts are also making it very difficult for councils to reinvest that money in building new homes. Setting a three-year limit for spending receipts, alongside a bizarre rule that they can only fund 30% of a development and can't be mixed with other grant funding, means councils cannot take a long-term approach and in some cases are simply having to hand that money back to the government. This cannot be right.

The government should also restrict tenants' Right to Buy rights on estates undergoing regeneration, which can delay projects for years as councils are forced into a lengthy and complex compulsory purchase order route that stops new homes being built quickly.

Do you think cross-subsidy will continue to be an effective way of funding new affordable housing?

Hackney's approach is unique in its simplicity – we build market sale homes to pay for the construction of new council homes for social rent and shared ownership, with a commitment that more than half will be for the latter. Part of the reason we are able to do that is the massive increase in land values in London, but it also requires a long-term, portfolio-wide approach that understands that some schemes will be unviable and therefore require subsidy from those that are more profitable.

As long as there continues to be no government funding for social housing, the arbitrary HRA borrowing cap remains and land values continue to rise, this is the only viable option for councils to fulfil their duty of directly building the thousands of new homes our country needs. We're keen to demonstrate that our approach is working – and instead of just talking about building new homes, we're actually delivering them. We're already seeing other councils interested in following our model and we really believe it can be an effective way of funding new genuinely affordable housing.

How is Hackney dealing with the need to provide employment/non-residential space in the borough?

The tension between building the thousands of homes we need to meet demand and the need to provide employment space for those people to work in is a growing concern in London.

Our estate regeneration schemes do not contribute to a loss in employment space, as we are building on council housing estate land rather than in industrial areas. But as land values and commercial rents rise, there is a risk that smaller firms in the borough will be forced elsewhere.

Hackney was one of the first boroughs to establish an approved affordable workspace providers' list to ensure that developers had access to competent, exciting and recognised providers who could deliver the kind of workspace we want to see in our borough, unlocking opportunities for new businesses and entrepreneurs. Our work with fantastic charities and social enterprises such as The Mill Co. Project and Bootstrap, has transformed thousands of square feet of space into effective places for the start-up businesses, cultural organisations and tech firms that give Hackney its reputation.

Safeguarding and delivering new affordable workspace outside of priority employment areas can be very difficult for planning authorities to implement, especially in areas with lower land value where viability may be more challenging. Unlike section 106 commitments around affordable housing, it is more difficult for local authorities to demand that quality affordable workspace that meets the needs of local business and growth sectors is provided

1.0.5 Model showing Hackney-led Colville Estate redevelopment

as part of development. We're working with the GLA to explore the options around this with other boroughs in the same position.

Could you go into more depth on the housing supply programme?

We've worked hard to ensure our estate regeneration programme is delivering thousands of homes to replace those that are uneconomical to repair. But it's clear that local authorities must make the most of the land they own to build new housing, even on estates where properties are in a good condition. Our housing supply programme does just that. On an initial 11 sites, such as old council depots and underused garages, we're planning to build more than 400 new homes, with at least 70% for social rent and shared ownership.

Local residents on these estates will get the first option to move into the new homes through a dedicated local lettings policy, while the programme will aim to recruit Hackney residents for a quarter of construction jobs.

We're keen not to build identikit homes that don't fit into their environment. Just because these are smaller projects, it shouldn't mean they don't get the same design input as larger schemes. We've put out tenders aimed at smaller, emerging architect practices who we want to challenge us with innovative design.

What is Hackney's strategy when looking forward to the mayor's ambition for 50% affordable housing?

Our estate regeneration model has demonstrated that you can deliver at least 50% affordable housing, and we believe this long-term, portfolio approach is the best way to deliver it, rather than focusing on each individual site and planning application.

Do you have much contact with other boroughs in terms of advice/expertise?

We regularly meet with our neighbouring boroughs to talk about our projects, share our challenges and successes and find out about best practice. We are also active members of organisations in London that promote development best practice, which are great ways to learn from other boroughs and the wider industry about good ideas happening elsewhere in the capital. Of course we also work closely with the GLA, and we think there is real potential for their enabling role to be expanded to assist boroughs with locally led delivery.

How important do you think it is for local authorities to retain as much public land as possible in order to develop long-term income streams, as opposed to short-term land disposal?

Parcelling off bits of land and selling them to the highest bidder is not an approach that creates viable, long-term affordable housing for London, and it does not provide the financial security needed to deliver vital local services. Eventually, the land will run out and so will the short-term income stream from sales that come with it.

We believe our long-term, 40-year approach is the right one because it is unapologetically a commercial approach but with a social purpose. It brings together a mix of historic failed schemes and sites that would be unviable on their own into an overarching programme, rather than selling each one off piecemeal.

And because we act as our own developer and have a skilled in-house direct delivery team, we don't need to rely completely on a private sector partner. That means we can retain our land, keep control of our assets, and collect rental income from the modern new homes we build for years to come. Knowing we have that long-term income stream means we can be bolder about the borrowing and investment decisions we make now, rather than seeking short-term gain.

What is Hackney doing to support local apprenticeships in housebuilding?

Regeneration can't just be about new bricks and mortar, which is why, when issuing tenders for projects, we make it a key requirement of all our partners to deliver apprenticeships and employ as much local labour as possible. Their response to these requirements forms part of our evaluation and makes a difference when we're deciding on who wins contracts.

For instance, at our Kings Crescent estate regeneration scheme in Stoke Newington, at least 25% of workers will be from Hackney, there will be nearly 50 apprentices on site, and we're aiming to ensure that as many as possible of those go on into long-term employment.

And at our Colville estate regeneration scheme, we've worked with the contractors to carry out a detailed skills audit of existing residents in order to understand what the challenges are for local people in finding work, and how we can connect them with employment and training programmes that exist locally – including the council's own Ways Into Work project. We'll continue to explore other ways in which we can use our schemes to support new life opportunities.

How important is the input of residents in Hackney's estate regeneration programme?

The involvement of residents is a vital part of any regeneration plan. Building modern new homes means huge upheaval for a whole community – moving house and putting up with years of construction. Our approach is to make local people integral to every part of the process – not just to win support for a masterplan, but because they will often have great ideas and understand their area better than council officers ever can.

At the Colville Estate, there was some mistrust between the council and residents because of a long history of previous attempts at regeneration that had failed due to partnerships falling through and funding issues. Understandably, promises of change fell flat and we faced a huge challenge to demonstrate that our new plans were different and that we meant it when we said we wanted residents to be involved. That trust was built up over years of masterplanning – through a dedicated steering group, many consultation events and feedback that showed directly how residents' ideas could feed into design. For instance, residents helped shape the design of two blocks of outright

sale housing that would help pay for all of the new council homes – not just the ones they'd be moving into. That partnership was cemented when construction started and they could see the results of their input. ■■■■

Karen Barke has worked in local authority urban regeneration and housing for over 15 years, and currently manages the estate regeneration programme at Hackney Council - one of the biggest schemes of its kind in the UK. Leading a skilled in-house team, Hackney Council's vison will deliver an innovative, council-led housebuilding programme of nearly 3,000 new homes at a range of tenures, alongside transformative economic and social benefits.

1.1
Colville Estate, UK
Karakusevic Carson Architects

Phase 1 + 2   Karakusevic Carson Architects + landscape by muf architecture/art
Phase 3   Karakusevic Carson Architects + David Chipperfield + VOGT Landscape Architects

Country	UK
Location	Hackney, London
Client	London Borough of Hackney
Cost	Phase 1 £6m, Phase 2 £45m, Phase 3 £60m
Funding	Local authority, cross-subsidy funding
Units	925
Scale	4-20 storeys
Density	225 d/ha
Mixed uses	Ground floor retail units and community centre
Tenures	Minimum of 42% social rent, 10% intermediate rent, 48% market sale (reviewable at each stage)
Key dates	Outline planning 2010, first phase completed 2012, phase 2 and 3 on site 2016
Procurement	Design and build. Design team employed by Hackney until Stage 4A tender. Design team novated to contractor after tender

1.1.0 Location plan, scale 1:5000

Prior to the current regeneration process now underway on the Colville Estate, the existing residents had been speaking to the council about regeneration for over 15 years. There had been three failed attempts at schemes to redevelop their deteriorating housing stock, but all had stalled at ballot and funding stages, the final one unravelling as a result of the financial crisis of 2007. In addition to fundamental building fabric and maintenance issues, the existing estate had suffered from poor original planning that resulted in an urban form that was inward-looking, with illegible block entrances and street patterns.

In 2010, the Karakusevic Carson led team was appointed by Hackney Council and submitted an outline planning application (OPA) for the comprehensive development of the estate. The OPA comprised full demolition of the existing buildings and outlined the new Colville neighbourhood as a series of development zones accommodating up to 925 units, of which approximately 50% will be social rent and shared ownership and 50% market sale. The demolition, relocation and construction period is anticipated to span a 15–20 year period.

During this process the residents established a very strong residents' charter with Hackney Council's support, which set out ground rules and non-negotiable points. It included a clear set of statements for the regeneration of the estate in terms of the design and implementation process, tenant involvement, management and aftercare and the nature of the replacement development.

Specifically, a large number of residents were opposed to being rehoused in tall buildings, but wanted low- and medium-rise homes ranging from four to six storeys. However, a scheme of average height and density would only generate about 600 homes, resulting in many tens of millions of pounds worth of funding shortfall, a disparity that was not going to be subsidised by central government. As a result, the design team began to investigate the possibility of increasing the density on a small part of the site – about 5% of the overall land – in order to create enough cross-subsidy to build all of the low- and medium-rise socially rented homes that would be required.

The architects suggested that an area of land on the south-western corner, facing the park, was a natural place for

1.1.1 Ground-floor plan, scale 1:1000

1.1.2 Proposed view of neighbourhood street

a series of bigger buildings. Following a series of meetings and design workshops with the residents' association, these denser blocks were incorporated into the masterplan and designated for shared ownership and market sale. Over 90% of the residents were supportive of the tall buildings because of the opportunities it gave for the wider estate to be built at a finer grain. Without the tall buildings, the whole estate would have been eight to nine storeys high – something that would not have been supported by the majority of existing residents. It is an exemplar of public consultation, involving weekly meetings with the residents' steering group to develop a phased, mixed-tenure masterplan and a specific aesthetic that could be agreed on by all.

1.1.3 Courtyard block section, scale 1:500

1.1.4 Flat plan of upper-level maisonette scale 1:200

1.1.5 Cutaway axonometric

The process of the regeneration of the Colville Estate is being carried out in a number of key phases:

Phase 1 Bridport House was completed in 2011, providing 41 new social rented units in two mid-level zero carbon buildings made from cross-laminated timber (CLT). The project is also one of the largest buildings in the world to use sustainable CLT technology.

Phase 2 was granted Reserved Matters Approval for 209 mixed tenure units in 2012 and is being developed in two sub phases of which one is currently in construction. It will provide a 'family' of medium-density, low-rise buildings of high-quality homes for existing and future residents, along with retail space, a community hub and energy centre. Improvements to the public realm aim to create a more liveable streetscape for residents, as well as connect the area to the wider neighbourhood.

Phase 3 is under construction at the time of publishing and is due for completion in 2018 – a 20-storey building and a 16-storey building providing up to 198 homes for market sale overlooking the park in the south-west corner of the estate. Arrived at after considerable consultation with local residents, the sale of homes in these two towers, designed as a collaboration between Karakusevic Carson Architects and David Chipperfield Architects, will help to cross subsidise the construction of affordable homes for the rest of the estate in its entirety.

The masterplan, which allows for increased density and financial viability through a mixture of tenancies, has been carried out in close conjunction with the residents and is representative of a positive and pragmatic housebuilding policy on the part of Hackney Council. In addition, it seeks to create a public realm strategy, stitching together the area and integrating it with the wider neighbourhood, providing for broader regeneration and renewal opportunities.

The residents' charter and the collaborative design processes were key to developing a viable regeneration strategy at the Colville Estate. The result is a clear spatial framework that achieves the density, streets and typologies that local residents wanted, supported by a complementary architectural scheme.

1.2
Agar Grove, UK
Hawkins\Brown + Mae

Country	UK
Location	Camden, London
Client	London Borough of Camden/the residents of Agar Grove Estate
Cost	£97m
Funding	London Borough of Camden
Units	497
Scale	Four-storey stacked maisonettes to 17-storey tower
Density	180 d/ha
Mixed uses	Workspace, retail, community centre
Tenures	240 market, 37 shared ownership, 216 social rent
Key dates	Planning granted August 2014, Phase 1a on site 2016
Procurement	Design and build with tender at Stage 4A

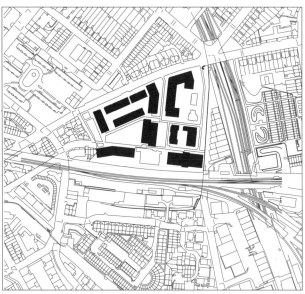

1.2.0 Location plan, scale 1:5000

Camden council's community investment programme (CIP) is a 15-year plan to invest money in schools, homes and community facilities. Reduced central government funding requires local authorities to be more innovative in making the best use of buildings and land to improve community facilities. Existing properties that are expensive to maintain, underused or difficult to access may be sold or redeveloped to generate funds that are not otherwise available to reinvest into improving services and facilities.

Design services for the redevelopment of Agar Grove were tendered through the Official Journal of the European Union (OJEU) process with a pre-qualification questionnaire and subsequent invitation to tender.. A team led by Hawkins\Brown, alongside Mae architects and Grant Associates, successfully bid for the job and were awarded the contract in December 2012. From the outset there was a collaborative ethos between Camden Council's CIP team and the design team. Public consultation was a key theme of the design process. It was crucial for the residents to be part of the process; their views were listened to and they were kept informed on progress and next steps.

Planning consent was granted in April 2014. The design team was retained by the client to prepare a tender package for the first phase of the works and was then part of the interview panel that assessed the tender returns. Hill Partnership was the successful bidder for the first phase of the works. Hawkins\Brown, Mae and Grant Associates have subsequently been retained by Camden Council as design guardians, a role that encompasses monitoring design quality and commenting on contractor design proposals to ensure design integrity in line with tender documents and employer's requirements. Phase 1a is currently on site and due for completion in 2017. Whilst the neighbourhood is a pleasant place to live, the existing layout of the estate does not compare well to today's principles of good urban design, reading as a series of objects which are dislocated from the wider city. The overarching design intent is to produce a scheme which is integrated into the local area. This is achieved by developing a masterplan based upon the traditional concept of streets and squares, with an emphasis on buildings which have front doors at street level, creating liveable

1.2.1 Location plan, scale 1:5000

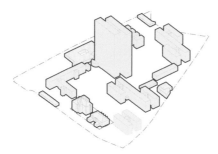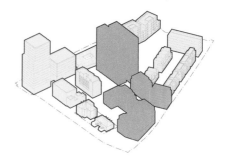

1.2.2 Phasing diagram

1.2.3 Communal core and maisonette entrance

spaces between them and allowing people to move across, through and within the site. The primary desire is to create a place where people want to live.

One of the principal objectives of the proposed redevelopment of Agar Grove is to rehouse existing residents once within the new scheme, to minimise disruption. The community has been established for over 40 years and this process will enable it to stay together. All existing residents have completed a Housing Need survey, identifying requirement, including size of residential unit and wheelchair use. This in turn has informed the unit type and mix of the proposals on a block-by-block basis.

Developed in Germany in the 1990s, Passivhaus is a "fabric-first" approach to designing low-energy buildings. The new-build Agar Grove homes will be built to achieve Passivhaus certification, which will dramatically reduce the

1.2.4 Aerial view of proposed massing

need for space heating and can cut heating bills by 90% compared with conventional homes. Key elements of Passivhaus include: super insulation, stringent airtightness, minimal thermal bridging, optimisation of passive solar gain, mechanical ventilation with heat recovery and high specification of windows and doors.

The area immediate to Agar Grove has a wide range of residential building typologies, which is representative of the wider London context. The typologies of terrace, villa, mansion block and tower have been identified and are employed within the Agar Grove masterplan as a way of connecting to the locality. Furthermore, these typologies provide a range of unit types for the varying needs of the residents and include family terrace housing and maisonettes with gardens, stepped level flats and lateral flats with balconies.

As part of the Agar Grove masterplan, Lulworth House, an existing 18-storey tower, will be retained, stripped back to its structure and intensively refurbished. The concrete structure in the building represents a significant amount of embodied carbon and retaining it for retrofitting is a large part of the sustainability strategy for the Agar Grove project. The process will be to remove internal partitions and the external cladding in order to strip the building back to its concrete skeleton. Then the central stair and lift core are also removed to open up a full-length corridor that is glazed at each end. New lifts and stairs will be provided in a new circulation core with dramatic views over the triangular park space to the west. Additional value will be added through the extension of the building both outward and upward, which will also improve the internal

spaces. The addition of sliding glass screens transforms the balcony areas into winter gardens. A central concierge will occupy part of the ground floor and will have views directly onto the street. Entrances on the east and west sides will connect right through the building so that the public space beyond can be clearly seen.

The public realm concept of streets and squares has been developed to provide a new urban fabric to the site, forging links with the local context and addressing the dead-end routes and poor connectivity of the existing estate. At the heart of the scheme a new garden square (Lulworth Gardens) provides a landscape of pedestrian and cycle priority circulation routes, play spaces, gardens and parks. Ground floor level access to individual residential units and blocks helps to activate the frontages of all buildings opening out onto the garden square and the adjoining new streets. The two character zones are defined by careful use of hard landscape materials such as paving and edge types, with higher-quality edge treatments being used in the garden square. The planting strategy is used to further strengthen the character of each space; trees have been used to bring a clear structure of mature canopy heights, which are supported by a planting palette that considers the scale, use and maintenance of each space.

This large-scale intervention demonstrates a series of successful strategies, including retaining existing homes, infill projects, demolition and extensive refurbishment of buildings. This is supported by a detailed landscape and public realm strategy that addresses the failings of the existing urban plan and creates a clear and stronger sense of place and differentiation.

1.2.5 Typical unit plan showing amendments, scale 1:200

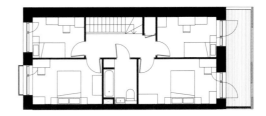

1.3
Silchester Estate, UK
Haworth Tompkins

Country	UK
Location	North Kensington, London
Client	Peabody and London Borough of Kensington and Chelsea
Cost	£24m
Funding	Local authority grant funding from RBKC and GLA
Units	112
Scale	1-9 storeys
Density	422 d/ha
Mixed uses	Retail unit 537 sq m, community spaces 537 sq m, landscaped garden 1,905 sq m
Tenure	45 social rent, 39 shared ownership and 28 private sale
Key dates	Start 2010, planning 2013, Phase 1 completed 2015, Phase 2 completed 2016
Procurement	Design and build. Design team employed by Peabody until Stage 4A tender. Design team novated to contractor after tender

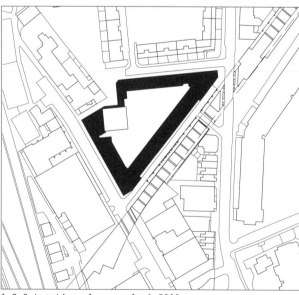

1.3.0 Location plan, scale 1:5000

Haworth Tompkins is working with Peabody and the Royal Borough of Kensington and Chelsea (RBKC) to implement a major regeneration project at the edge of the Silchester estate, adjacent to Latimer Road tube station. The Silchester Estate, typically of post-war housing projects, sought to restructure the historic city, providing high-rise blocks set in an open landscape combined with more traditional terraces of low-rise housing. Access is via cul-de-sacs that isolate the estate, rather than via streets that would help link it with the adjacent streetscape.

The redevelopment scheme is designed around a new communal garden, integrating an existing 20-storey tower block, and providing family homes for social rent alongside shared ownership and apartments for sale. The new urban block reinforces the character of existing residential street patterns, animating corners with community spaces and retail, and creating a new mews alongside the existing railway arches which will be opened up for commercial use.

Most of the development is four to five storeys, consistent with the scale of the surrounding area. The scale increases at the two prominent mews street corners, where each block is crowned with a rooftop pavilion set back from the main façade. The highest nine-storey block provides a distinctive feature to hold the corner of the site and helps to mediate between the scale of the new block and the existing tower, Frinstead House. A two-storey community centre facing Freston Road physically connects with the existing tower. The façade seamlessly envelops the tower at the lower level, reconfiguring and upgrading its entrance to tie in with the overall scheme's palette of materials.

The qualities of Peabody's existing 19th-century housing estates, along with the terrace house typology, are the reference points for the choice of materials and details. Two tones of brick are used, a rich buff brick predominates, and lighter creamy/white "gault" brick is used where the blocks are set back at higher levels. Openings have a vertical emphasis, with regular repeated proportions creating a horizontal and vertical rhythm characteristic of traditional London housing.

1.3.1 Location plan, scale 1:1000

All residential units are dual aspect with optimal levels of daylight. Large external balconies are either recessed on the street frontages or project over the communal garden within. Private terraces for the ground-floor family units provide a buffer between the private residences and the shared garden. Designed as a lush open green space to look onto and move freely within, the garden is accessible to all residents of the scheme. Natural play opportunities have been integrated within the landscape.

This scheme will provide many new homes on the edge of an existing estate and a strong community. The architects undertook significant consultation to gain valuable input and to ensure that local people have had a positive contribution to the scheme's development. In particular, they have changed the scheme to ensure that those residents who will be rehoused into the new development will remain together on the ground floor,

with generous private gardens connected by a private path to the rear and shielded with planting from the communal garden.

Community benefits include a new social enterprise hub, a space for young entrepreneurs to develop their businesses. Other facilities include a community space, modifications to the Silchester residents' club room and a retail unit proposed opposite the tube station. This will signal the entrance to the mews, and link to the existing shops. A new landscape design for a park to the north of the site will open up the new development to the existing estate. This is an important part of the proposal, ensuring that local residents benefit from the investment in the new scheme. Working in partnership with the enlightened client group, the architects for this project have successfully delivered an integrated urban scheme and high-quality architectural solution.

1.3.2 View of new street frontage

1.3.3 View of communal courtyard

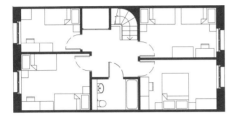

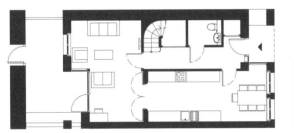
1.3.4 Flat plan of maisonette scale 1:200

1.3.5 Aerial view of completed urban block integrating retained tower

1.4
Goldsmith Street, UK
Mikhail Riches

Country	UK
Location	Norwich
Client	Norwich City Council
Cost	£15m
Funding	Norwich City Council
Units	105
Scale	2-3 storeys
Density	83 d/ha
Tenures	100% social housing (50% houses, 50% flats)
Key dates	Start on site January 2017, completion May 2018
Procurement	Framework with competitive tender at Stage 4A

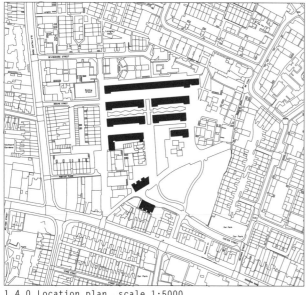

1.4.0 Location plan, scale 1:5000

Norwich City Council is embarking on one of the UK's most ambitious, state-led sustainable supply-chain frameworks in order to deliver homes built to the highest European energy standards. Adopting the "fabric-first" approach, the framework will be used by the local authority but will also be available to all UK public sector bodies and registered social landlords (RSLs). Norwich City Council is keen to exceed the standards required by the building regulations, both for environmental reasons and as part of a drive to reduce fuel poverty. The framework provides a resource of contractors who have the skills and expertise to build to Passivhaus standards. It will be used for a range of projects, working with both traditional and design and build contracts. The council is currently working on three housing projects, providing in total 287 homes, with all but 50 designed to the Passivhaus standard.

One of the new housing schemes being brought forward using the "fabric-first" framework is Goldsmith Street by Mikhail Riches. It is a high-density scheme for the area, with 105 properties – a mix of one-, two-, three- and four-bedroom houses and flats, 100% of which will be available for social rent. The project was originally won through an RIBA-led competition by Riches Hawley Mikhail in 2008. It had been the city's intention to sell the site to a local RSL, with the design team and the scheme ideas agreed beforehand. However, with the onset of the financial crisis of 2008, the development stalled, as the local RSLs were unable to make the scheme work financially due to funding cuts. Various alternative proposals were presented to the local authority by RSLs, but Norwich city planning department was not receptive to any of them. In 2014 the city decided to develop the site itself, without a housing association or development partner. It then appointed the architects directly and asked them to develop the original competition scheme. Consequently, the client from RIBA Stage 2 onwards has been Norwich City Council.

Located within a mile of Norwich city centre, the Goldsmith Street site is bounded by medium- and low-rise, 1970s local-authority housing. The proposal reintroduces a terraced street pattern into this area of the city, which had been blighted by amorphous estates of high- and low-rise

Second-floor plan

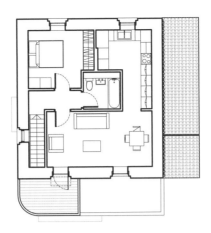

First-floor plan

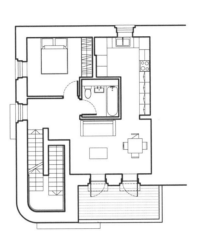

Ground-floor plan

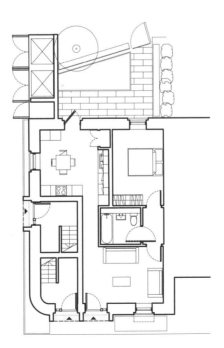

1.4.1 Typical flat plan, scale 1:200

1.4.2 Proposed view towards new neighbourhood street

1.4.3 Proposed view of shared private back gardens

flats since 1945. These proposed streets establish new pedestrian, cycle routes and green links, reinforced with a landscape scheme which extends beyond the boundaries of the site. Street widths are intentionally narrow, emulating the popular 19th century terraced streets nearby, known locally as the Golden and Silver Triangles. With similar distances between façades of 14 metres, the architects demonstrated to Norwich City Council that these new homes would overcome some of the overlooking issues present in the later Edwardian streets nearby.

This scheme demonstrates how local authority managed projects can take a longer-term view of running costs, investing more in the building fabric initially in order to minimise the risks of fuel poverty for tenants. The design seeks to provide sunny, light-filled homes with very low fuel bills of approximately £150 per year. Through the introduction of streets running east to west, the vast majority of habitable rooms face south, overshadowing

between properties is minimised with shallow 25-degree roof pitches, with unusually low eaves on the north side of 4.8 metres. The project has been carefully detailed to eliminate cold-bridging; external walls are 625mm thick to achieve adequate insulation levels. In addition to thermal performance in winter, solar shading prevents overheating in summer.

Existing green links are to be reinforced with a landscape scheme, which extends beyond the boundaries of the site to include local roads and a park. With the aspiration for the project to address the adjoining areas where appropriate, two small sites on neighbouring streets are to be included in the overall development to strengthen important existing connections. It also incorporates landscape improvements to existing green spaces, improving pedestrian access through the neighbourhood, creating well-lit and clearly defined routes. A shared "alley", encouraging small children's play and communal gathering, is accessible from back gardens – a secure place which only keyholders (residents) can access.

The proposed scheme is dense and low rise, providing approximately 50 individual houses and 50 flats. Generous kitchen and dining rooms form the heart of each house. The scheme has been designed with no internal common parts, so every dwelling has its own front door opening directly onto the street at ground level, with its own dedicated hallway and staircase up to either first or second floors. This device allows private and social tenures to be mixed across the site, whilst also playing a part in keeping maintenance costs and anti-social behaviour to a minimum.

This project demonstrates that outside London, working within a constrained economic context, Norwich Council is committed to improving housing quality. Through a lifetime costing approach, it is investing more than a developer would, in order to meet ambitious sustainability targets that are integrated into the procurement, urbanism and architectural designs. The scheme also responds to residents' priorities and achieves a greater density than typical of the locality, through intelligent design of housing typologies.

Interview
Jeremy Grint + Jennifer Coombes
London Borough of Barking & Dagenham

How is the Barking and Dagenham council housing programme funded?

Barking has delivered around 1,000 new homes over the past five years, some of which is council housing of the traditional kind and some of which has been developed through other means. In terms of funding, there is a fund allocated specifically for housing, and a general fund which should not be used for housing but can be used for capital projects. In addition to this, we have benefited from European Investment Bank funding, which can only be spent on affordable housing. We are currently working on an estate renewal scheme of 1,500 homes on the edge of the town centre, where Barking will take all the affordable rent while another company will take on the shared ownership element. There is a general tendency towards shared ownership as a borough, which is currently more popular politically than market rented housing.

The council has a number of small sites, disused garages etc, which can be used for infill purposes. We also work with partners such as TfL, GLA etc, to develop land for housing as part of our own in-house regeneration team, which is made up of around seven individuals. These range from asset management schemes to estate renewals and working out how to manage our projects efficiently.

The majority, if not all, of Barking's regeneration schemes have been built on brownfield land. Does this tend to mean that development depends more on private investment to develop this land?

Not really, as the land that we develop ourselves is funded by our rent model. By charging a slightly higher affordable rent band – although still affordable for most ordinary people – we are able to help fund development in the borough. We have three main bands: 50% market rent (a social rent equivalent), 65% and 80%, which are only targeted at people in stable full-time employment. All three fall under the heading of "affordable" housing, which shows that the term has a wide variety of meanings.

Some central London boroughs have employed a policy of cross-subsidisation in order to fund estate regeneration schemes. Is that something Barking has the ability to pursue?

This is definitely more of a central London trend; we don't have the benefit of rapidly rising values to do this. Our cross-subsidy comes from our rent model and balancing our band levels to accommodate the complexities of each scheme.

The idea of social housing is far removed from its original definition to incorporate other more complex tenure types. How has this affected provision of local authority housing in Barking and Dagenham?

The terminology has changed dramatically. When I started working in housing it was relatively straightforward – social rent, shared ownership, intermediate rent, private sale, etc. Now there are so many sub-categories, like capped rent, discounted rent, affordable rent and shared equity, which makes the consultation process especially difficult.

Could you give a brief background to the William Street Quarter scheme?

Back in 2007–08 we were looking at several estate renewal plans which had particularly challenging layouts. The blocks were enclosed deck-access, which had become dangerous over time, given the fact they were being increasingly blocked up as storage areas. Even at that time, the cost of renovating the units was costed at around £60,000 per unit. It was deemed that refurbishment was not the most efficient solution and the decision was made to demolish 257 units. Central government funding for the scheme dried up and we were left to find alternative methods of financing the project. Eventually, a special purpose vehicle (SPV) was set up, known as Reside, with a 60-year rental guarantee, after which time the land would be returned to the council as freeholders. William Street Quarter was carried out this way, working with Alford Hall Monaghan Morris and Maccreanor Lavington architects. In total, 232 units were provided, all at

1.0.6 Anne Mews, Barking, the first new
      council housing built in Barking
      and Dagenham for 25 years

1.0.7 Barking town centre, a key piece
      of new public realm

1.0.6

1.0.7

affordable rent. The local authority delivered 31 units directly and the rest through Reside, a local-authority run RSL providing housing at 80% of the market rate.

Barking is generally a low-rise borough. Is there much scope for different typologies or heights?

There is room for high-rise development, particularly in the area directly around the station. The Gascoigne Estate masterplan, for example, ranges from two to 12 storeys, providing 1,575 homes, 55% of which are affordable.

What do you see as the main solution to unlocking housing supply in London?

There is the whole issue of the construction industry in general with price inflation in recent years and also the availability of resources. There's been a huge move in London towards brick as a material, away from the panel systems of 10 years ago. Contractors therefore are finding there is a skills gap in this line of work, which raises prices. For me, we are moving more towards modular construction, which benefits the larger housing providers who have the ability to take on large amounts of risk in the long term. Any scheme that has a timescale of beyond the next four years or so will be costed to allow for fluctuations in the market.

We are now faced with a problem in that the cost of construction is so high that affordable rent alone doesn't stack up financially.

The Barking Riverside project has been characterised by its relative lack of infrastructural connections. How does the provision of transport connections tie in with regeneration in the borough?

Eight hundred homes, and by the end of this year the figure will be 1,200. A detailed planning application will go in this year. In late 2017 to early 2018, high-density development will go on site with a view to linking in with the opening of the station in 2021. Now that London and Quadrant (L&Q) has taken over from a private developer, there is an expectation that the number of homes will increase year on year. All units are expected to be completed by 2031. The railway extension is funded by L&Q, TfL and the GLA. This process is part of a joint venture between L&Q and the GLA, which provides serviceable land to housebuilders. Originally a Docklands Light Railway (DLR) extension was proposed to Barking riverside; however, this was then shelved.

At some point along the line, councils were no longer able to borrow money to fund their own housing schemes. Do you see this changing at all?

Even since the 1980s, councils became so constrained with what we could do that housing development stopped completely. Until 2008 when we started our new housebuilding programme, new building in Barking was at a standstill. Anne Mews was the first council housing built in Barking for 25 years.

In 2012, the government changed things which meant councils could borrow again. However, there was a value allocated to each borough based on the income derived from its housing stock. This refinancing policy meant that some boroughs had much higher "headroom" than others. Hackney, for example, had around £100m which could be used for housing, while in Barking we had only around £8m.

This was also determined by historic debt, which each borough had accumulated over time, and this affected its own ability to borrow. Another way to put this in context is to look at Right to Buy – before this policy we had a housing stock of 47,000 units and now it is around 18,000.

What is the future for Barking and Dagenham council, and what are the restrictions which need to be overcome?

The main factor which is holding back development is land assembly. As a borough we simply do not have much spare land that can be used for development. One way of doing this is estate renewal, but through the policies of Right to Buy, this is problematic in terms of repaying leaseholders and the complications of rehousing into new homes. The most straightforward way to develop is physically to go and buy up pieces of land. Some councils are already doing this in other boroughs or outside London.

One area which is particularly contentious is the use of grants. Since 2008 we have had an affordable housing programme with the investment partner being the GLA, which is now the main funder for affordable housing provision in London. Now we have to use our Right to Buy receipts for one-to-one replacements. We can't double count on the affordable housing programme grants and the Right to Buy receipts; we have to use one or the other. So in order to avoid losing these receipts and handing money back to government, we are left without an affordable housing programme. ■■■■■■

Jeremy Grint was the head of regeneration and economic development at the London Borough of Barking and Dagenham until 2016, having been responsible for physical town planning and economic regeneration for the last 13 years. He has led on major housing developments and mixed-use schemes in town centres and large brownfield sites, including Barking Riverside, and has 30 years' experience in both development activity and policy planning in the public sector. Most recently he was instrumental in the setup of the council's Reside housing company, delivering over 600 new affordable homes for the borough.

Jennie Coombs leads the housing regeneration team at the London Borough of Barking and Dagenham, working on design, development, implementation and managing a wide range of major housing, and housing-led mixed-use projects and programmes, including the council's estate renewal programme. She has over 30 years' experience in the housing sector, working in strategy, management and development, and she was recognised in the Building Construction Industry Awards 2015 for her role as client for two major affordable housing schemes.

2.1
Tour Bois-le-Prêtre, France
Lacaton & Vassal + Druot

2.2
Ellebo Garden Room, Denmark
Adam Khan Architects

2.3
Knikflats, The Netherlands
biq/Hans van der Heijden

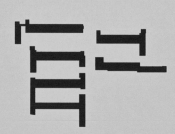

2.4
Hillington Square, UK
Mae

Renovation
strategies

2

Introduction

Across Europe the rehabilitation of large-scale estates is a common concern, with the living conditions in many of those built during the mid-20th century now far removed from their utopian origins. The reasons for deterioration are numerous and the scale of the problem varies from country to country. For some it is simply wear and tear or poor management and maintenance over many decades, for others though it is a fundamental problem of design, construction layout or urban integration. Uniting all, however, is the need to realise the potential of existing building stock and improve its long-term use in a sustainable way, as wholesale removal is not viable or desirable.

In the immediate post-war years an urgent need for housing and a scarcity of materials encouraged great innovation, and advanced building techniques were embraced. Architects and designers of the age provided buildings that responded to the challenge using approaches that provided a record number of dwellings. However, government targets, mass production and a focus on speed frequently led to poor workmanship and shoddy construction. Today our need for new housing is similar, but the scarcity of our current age is in land, and particularly land in the right location. Therefore innovation is again required in how we get the most out of it for the most people, without undermining quality or destroying communities.

Demolition was once the default strategy of those wanting to renovate an area and usher in change. In the 1950s, unpopular Victorian terraces were knocked down, while 30 years later failed post-war tower blocks were spectacularly blown up with triumphalist footage of it shown on television. Such simplistic approaches caused upheaval and were hugely wasteful. Many condemned estates at this time had failed as a result of years of underinvestment and a basic lack of regular maintenance. In other cases they were destroyed out of sheer disdain for what they represented socially, regardless of their design qualities or their ability to be thoughtfully or creatively rehabilitated.

The 1990s saw a wave of short-term remedial projects. Responding to new environmental performance criteria, many cash-strapped authorities and housing associations were forced into undertaking light-touch refurbishments. Expedient engineering overtook the idea of place-making and while conceived with the best intentions, the results tended towards cheap cladding systems mutilating building stock, reducing window openings, restricting ventilation and impairing drainage. In tandem, other refurbishment programmes were rolled out, driven by a fear of crime and vandalism. The result was the increasing securitisation of estates with shared spaces removed and the application of bollards, fences, railings and a range of largely cosmetic niceties that did little to improve their function or fundamentally change living conditions.

Nuanced and considered strategies are now being adopted all over Europe, which recognise architectural quality, tackle the performance of building stock and rethink the use of public space. Conceived through discussion and collaboration with resident populations, the projects featured in this chapter explore enlightened and long-term approaches to refurbishment that include a mixture of partial demolition, infill and building adaptation. Recurring themes include improving thermal performance, redefining communal access and circulation areas, extending private outdoor space, activating ground floors and clarifying the relationship between private and public realms. ▬▬▬

2.0.1

Le Havre, by Auguste Perret, 1945-1964
Devastated during the second world war, the
reconstruction of the city of Le Havre was one of
Europe's great modern projects. Perret's bold vision
for a new urban core provided new commercial premises,
civic buildings, amenity space and, crucially, housing,
80% of which had been lost during bombing campaigns.
New homes were provided through a refined and highly
desirable apartment block typology, which today defines
nearly all of Le Havre's post-war streets.

2.0.2

**Lea View House, Springfield Road, Hackney, London,
by Hunt Thompson Associates, 1989**
Originally built in the 1950s, this building of 300
dwellings was regarded as a slum just 20 years later.
After a local campaign, the local authority chose
to refurbish the block rather than demolish it, and
architects moved on site and worked with tenants to
revitalise the block, introducing secure areas and
character features.

2.0.3

**Holly Street Estate, London,
by Levitt Bernstein (various phases) 1992-2011**
Built between 1966 and 1971, by the 1990s this estate
was in urgent need of repair and was synonymous with
crime. Composed of four imposing towers and a series
of long and uncompromising "snake" blocks, the estate
was transformed through a holistic regeneration process
that saw almost total demolition and the introduction
of intimate streets and "humane" residential blocks.
Holly Street Estate was one of the first large-scale
public/private partnership projects in the UK.

2.0.4

**Park Hill, Sheffield.
Phase 1 by Hawkins\Brown and Studio Egret West, 2013**
The Grade II*-listed Park Hill estate is one of the
UK's great icons of Brutalism and was built between
1957 and 1961 by Sheffield city council. Influenced
by Le Corbusier's *Unité d'habitation* and new ideas of
streets in the sky, it was in a dilapidated state by
the 2000s. Its refurbishment stripped back the building
to its gridded concrete frame and introduced new
façades with modern glazing and simple, bright coloured
panels for new mixed-tenure living units.

Essay
Anne Lacaton: Transforming, reinventing
Founding partner at Lacaton & Vassal

2.0.5

2.0.6

2.0.7

Modern housing is often criticised, stigmatised and rejected. Regularly, this negative judgment is made from a distance by people who don't actually live in the project. It is undeniable that many of the grands ensembles find themselves in difficult situations and that the quality of life that they provide is much lower than what was imagined when they were constructed. Built on a massive scale in the 1960s and 1970s, they are now providing inadequate and unsatisfying living conditions, and in every city we are forced to question their future.

However, many of them possess potential quality; sometimes this quality needs to be revealed, developed, complemented and transcended by looking at housing from the inside rather than the outside, from up-close rather than from a distant perspective. The structural, geographical and spatial potential of these buildings is very often a useful starting point for the dramatic improvement of living standards and for the introduction of diversity that can be of economic and social benefit, and in the process add to the density of the existing housing.

Many of these projects possess the requirements for their own reimagining: transparency, unobstructed views, height, green space and existing fabric. It is no longer a matter of asking ourselves if the design of those housing projects was a mistake. They can be understood to be part of our heritage and of our contemporary history. Where it is possible, we must accept them, live with them and do what is necessary to enable them to evolve and to endure in changing times.

As firm believers in the capacity of this modern heritage, we are directly involved in this conversation, and have been for a long time. We have been working on the subject for more than 10 years, during which time the French government has embarked on a nationwide programme for urban renovation of the social grands ensembles. It was based on the complete deconstruction of those projects; the demolition and reconstruction of 150,000 to 200,000 homes. The programme was significant in its scale, the amount of money that was to be invested and the speed with which it would be implemented.

To qualify all housing projects of the period as a failure seemed unjustified to us, and the demolition a brutal, unilateral and unfounded decision. We decided that it was necessary to embark on an intensive study and analysis, in order to develop a detailed understanding which would enable us to propose alternative solutions. Collaborating with Frédéric Druot, with whom we had been sharing the same vision for some time, we decided to carry out this in-depth analysis on some specific cases. The aim of this study was to change the approach, clarify the diagnosis and to explain the circumstances in which complete redevelopment was not the right solution, and where an alternative transformative approach would be more appropriate for the particular estate and its residents. We felt that this approach could be more ambitious and sustainable, as well as being more realistic, efficient and far more economical than demolition.

The starting point for this study was an attitude: first and foremost we would investigate the neighbourhoods and their architecture with a fresh and positive eye. Instead of looking at the towers and slab blocks from a distance, condemning them for their poor appearance, we would look at them from the inside. By looking carefully around us and listening to the residents, we would make a precise inventory of what was relevant and what was not. We chose to start from the living space and to decide how it could be improved, extended, unfolded, expanding its scope and quality and to open it up towards the outside, releasing the common areas of the buildings in the process.

The study was conducted with Druot and published under the title *PLUS*. It supported a specific position: "Never demolish, never subtract or replace, always add, transform and use, complement, update and start from the existing in order to make more and better."

Transformation of the existing requires making the most of what is already there, making it more generous, giving more space to each resident, creating new opportunities and producing sustainable living conditions that will no longer be determined simply by the minimum economic, regulatory or legislative logics but by generosity and pleasure. It should include:

- more space that will improve living quality, such as balconies, terraces and transparency
- the enhancement of thermal comfort and the reduction in energy use

- lowering the population density within the existing buildings in order to reduce the feeling of congestion, but increasing the density around buildings to create new homes and add to the overall density
- offering new typologies, services, uses and shopping facilities.

Each of the studies that have been investigated has convinced us that transformation has the potential to be a more affordable, efficient and better quality response to the current need. It must be driven from the interior, the lived experience rather than the external form. We don't look at buildings as blocks, but as a set of situations and individual spaces that each family uniquely makes its own. ▬▬▬

Anne Lacaton founded the practice Lacaton & Vassal with partner Jean Philippe Vassal in Paris in 1987. Refurbishment and sensitive renovation are recurring themes in a wide ranging portfolio of projects across Europe that includes residential, cultural and commercial buildings.

2.0.5 Quartier du Grand Parc, Bordeaux, view of modified rear elevation

2.0.6 Quartier du Grand Parc, Bordeaux, façade before and after modification

2.0.7 Quartier du Grand Parc, Bordeaux, interior before and after modification

2.1
Tour Bois-le-Prêtre, France
Lacaton & Vassal + Druot

Country	France
Location	17TH ARR. Paris
Client	Paris Habitat
Cost	€11.2m
Funding	Public
Units	96
Scale	16 storeys
Tenures	100% social housing
Key dates	2005-2011

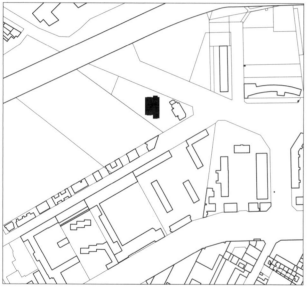

2.1.0 Location plan, scale 1:5000

The Tour Bois-le-Prêtre is arguably the best known European example of successful estate management and renovation. Using an intelligent technical approach to establish which elements of a building to remove and which to be retained, Lacaton & Vassal and Frédéric Druot have developed a strategy for a new way of dealing with existing social housing stock.

Built in 1961 on the edge of the 17th arrondissement of Paris, the original concrete frame tower was designed by the prolific and respected architect Raymond Lopez. The building was refurbished poorly at the beginning of the 1980s, dealing only with external works in isolation. Paying little attention to the internal qualities of the homes, the intervention actually worsened the residents' living space as well as the architectural composition of the building: window sizes were reduced, natural light and views diminished, loggias enclosed, ground floor pilotis blocked up, entrances narrowed and common areas removed.

Twenty years later, the building and its refurbishments became outdated once more. The previous renovation works hadn't added any long-term quality and a new restoration was needed. A typical process of total demolition and reconstruction was considered. However, the landowner, the social housing provider Paris Habitat, ran a competition to renovate the building. One of the principle constraints was that the building could not be expanded to take up more land: any renovation would need to keep to the building's existing footprint.

The intervention proposed by Lacaton & Vassal and Druot was founded on two major principles resulting from their collaborative study *PLUS*:

- the project had to start within the internal structure of the buildings to maximise quality and sustainability for each home
- the project would be carried out without moving residents, so that the transformation was actually focused with their direct benefit in mind. This required a specific type of construction technique and programme methodology.

The architects proposed simple but effective extensions: giving each home more internal space, adding

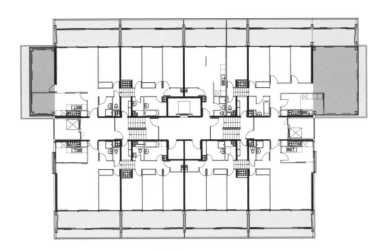

Extensions: winter garden
Extensions: heated extensions
Circular Core: north / south

2.1.1 Typical plan, before and after modification, scale 1:500

2.1.2 Original façade

2.1.3 Additional winter gardens and balconies

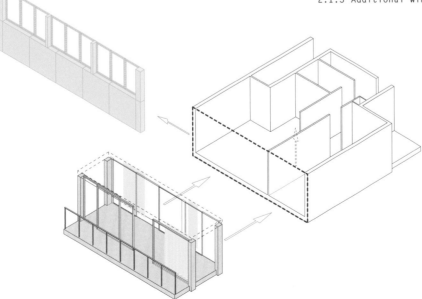

2.1.4 Axonometric of modification process

balconies or winter gardens, and improving comfort by restoring the light and the view that had been lost. Through an extension of 3 metres on each floor, all flats were extended by between 22 and 60 sq m by the provision of winter gardens, balconies or living areas. The layouts were reworked by changing the internal partitions and installing new kitchens and bathrooms, adding lobbies and new lifts. The intelligent use of prefabricated winter gardens and balconies meant that connecting a new module to a home would only take one day per apartment; the prefabricated winter gardens were craned into place at a rate of one unit per day, meaning disruption was kept to a minimum. Corrugated aluminium panels are typical of a palette of materials chosen in response to limits of the construction budget and a general approach of prioritising the internal experience, as opposed to focusing resources on the façade.

Heating energy levels were halved, thanks to the thermal performance of the winter gardens. Rents were maintained at their original level with no increase after the transformation. The financial cost of the restoration works is estimated to be half of the alternative demolition and reconstruction cost. The complete renovation works took a total of two years from start to finish, which also poses an attractive alternative to the time normally taken for a full demolition and rebuilding of existing estates for both residents and providers.

Lacaton & Vassal and Druot's research into this topic was begun more than a decade ago, but it remains a challenge to the norms of the architect's remit and brings into question the existing methodologies for intervening with estate regeneration projects. Using a relatively simple set of materials and prioritising the generosity of the internal spaces over nuanced detailing, the architects offer an alternative way of dealing with the economic realities of housing today. As an office, they have introduced a model that not only attempts to limit the social costs of displacing residents, but is also grounded in a pragmatism backed up by technical and financial evidence.

2.1.5 1980s recladding

2.1.6 Façade following modification

2.1.7 Section, before and after modification, scale 1:500

2.1.8 Winter garden, interior view

2.2
Ellebo Garden Room, Denmark
Adam Khan Architects

Country	Denmark
Location	Ballerup, Copenhagen
Client	KAB
Cost	DKK 247,000,000
Funding	Landsbyggefonden / KAB
Units	276
Scale	5 storeys
Density	60 d/ha
Tenures	100% social housing
Key dates	Start on site 2017, project completion 2019
Procurement	Traditional form of contract, with full detailed construction drawings – equivalent to RIBA Stage 4

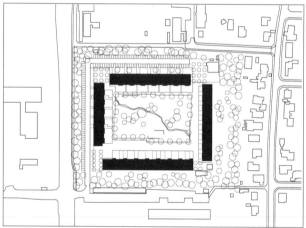

2.2.0 Location plan, scale 1:5000

A discourse of poor transport links, insufficient maintenance or funding and socio-economic issues are commonly identified in the initial analysis of post-war housing estates, leading to simplistic conclusions and often demolition. Ellebo, however, is in fact well located, with good local schools and only a 30-minute train journey from Copenhagen Central Station. It does, however, suffer from a monoculture of housing types and poorly defined public spaces. A superficial renovation of the estate in the 1980s added a layer of colour without addressing these fundamental issues.

In 2012, an architectural competition to redevelop the estate was launched by Nordic Innovation, an initiative set up to prototype sustainable approaches to the reuse of post-war industrialised housing. The winning proposal by Adam Khan Architects offers a radical approach, working at different scales and challenging prevalent models of regeneration. Intelligent strategic decisions are made across the site, for example confining new units to a single block rather than distributing them across the site as a way of economising construction costs. The proposal seeks to retain as much of the built fabric as possible and to reorientate living spaces towards the underutilised central garden. This has been achieved by extending the existing buildings in length and height to increase density and diversify the accommodation available, providing greater enclosure and better defining the character of the central garden.

More flexible refurbished dual-aspect flats are created by the use of modern methods of prefabrication and careful micro-surgery of the existing internal layouts. Removal of partitions creates a series of connected rooms forming new open layouts connected to the winter gardens and balconies, which in turn face onto the framed garden rooms and across to the other balconies. Crucially, the existing residents are able to remain in their homes throughout the process, as the prefabrication of panels allows for the façade system to be removed and replaced within two to four days.

The new façades are highly insulated, simple and economic. They are given a new hierarchy whereby the outer elevations are treated simply, whilst those facing the

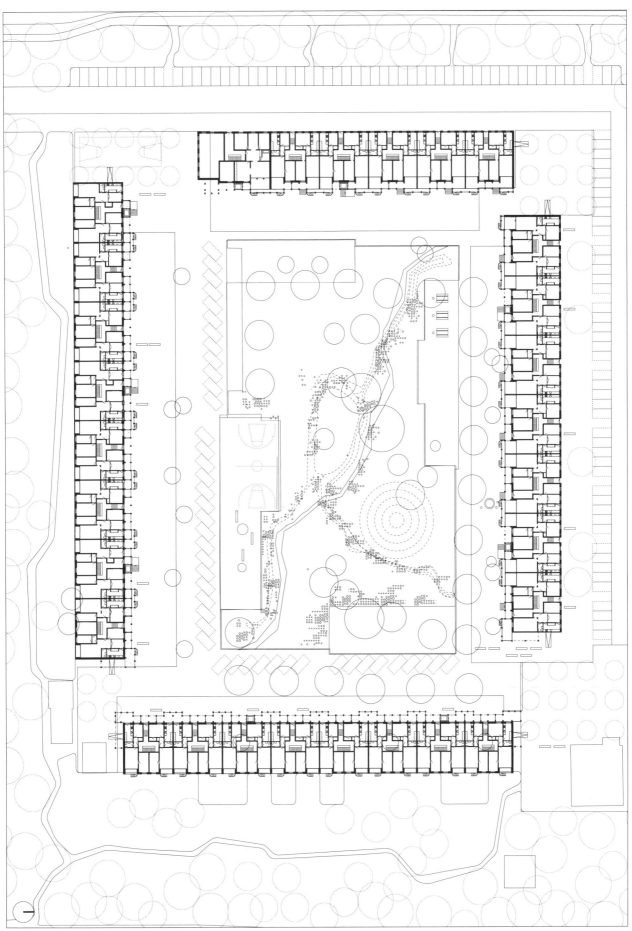

2.2.1 Ground-floor plan, scale 1:1000

2.2.2 Courtyard view prior to modifications

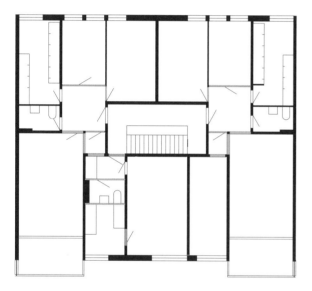

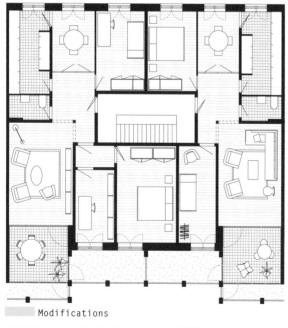

■ Modifications

2.2.3 Typical flat plan, scale 1:200

shared garden are celebrated by new winter gardens and balconies. These deliver high environmental performance in a simple and robust way, but also give the residents new seasonally flexible rooms. The new balconies are vertically proportioned, articulated into bays and made of robust precast concrete, forming a dignified, elegant backdrop for the social life of the estate. New lifts and direct access to the garden from all communal stairwells are integrated within this deep structure.

The shared garden will be allowed to adapt over time and, with the garden rooms, will enable overlapping activities and the increased contact desirable in public space. An energetic process of resident engagement will transform the shared landscape from a barren municipal green into a successfully appropriated and diverse set of gardens, by offering opportunities to unleash and cultivate the sense of ownership often suppressed in public housing. Cars and tarmac are reduced within the square by relocating parking to the outside edges.

Going far beyond the colourful reclad of the 1980s, the vision for the estate is as a place where young families will want to live, to stay and to form rich intergenerational bonds seen in successful housing. The choice to introduce bigger flats, often in the form of duplexes, will encourage families to move to the estate and alter the current demographic mix. The offer of affordable high-quality accommodation and the chance to express individuality and take initiative in the care of the shared spaces taps into contemporary desires of living well and living with others.

Too often the many problems associated with post-war housing estates can be conflated into toxic rhetoric that can cause their demise. The simple act of assessing and valuing that which already exists is a radical critique of tabula rasa redevelopment, bringing the myriad benefits of a sustainable approach from reduced embodied energy and reduced social upheaval, to conferring a sense of dignity and providing homes that are delightful and durable. This fundamentally changes the economic and emotional strains of the rehousing process which plagues so many estate regeneration projects.

2.2.4 Proposed view of new external access route

2.2.5 Living space before modification

2.2.6 Proposed view of living space after modification

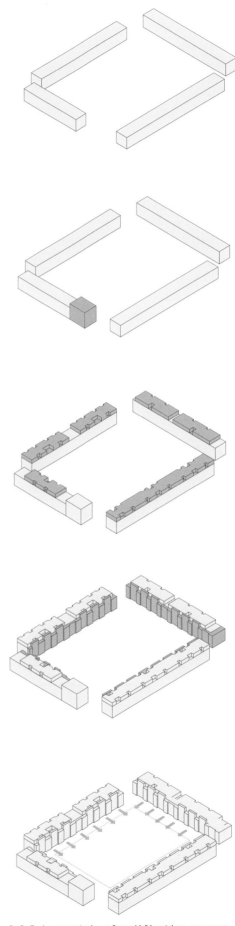

2.2.7 Axonometric of modification process

2.3
Knikflats, Ommoord, The Netherlands
biq / Hans van der Heijden

Country	Netherlands
Location	Ommoord, Rotterdam
Client	Woonbron Prins Alexander
Cost	€40m
Funding	Housing association - direct delivery
Units	704
Scale	8 storeys
Density	65 d/ha
Mixed use	Commercial and communal spaces
Tenures	50% affordable, 50% market sale
Key dates	Commission 1999, start on site 2006, completion 2009
Procurement	Tender after preliminary selection of contractors at Stage 4 equivalent

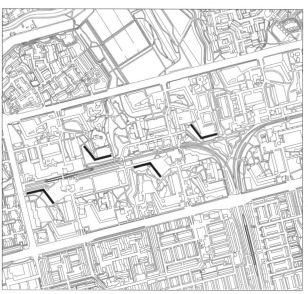

2.3.0 Location plan, scale 1:20000

Much of Rotterdam was in a state of ruin following the second world war, presenting a major urban planning challenge. One district newly created in the post-war period is that of Ommoord, on the northern outskirts of the city, designed by Bauhaus urban planner Lotte Stam-Besse, working in direct response to the severe housing shortage. Built in 1968, the district was built to house 35,000 people at a variety of scales and densities within a landscape setting. The denser part of the district was constructed as a series of high-rise slab blocks to accommodate a typically low-income community. biq's scheme dealt with four out of a total of 15 similar eight-storey blocks which required renovation and updating. The estate's size means that any intervention with an individual block is also a strategic response to the whole, with the architect becoming a strategic member of the estate management team.

Demolition was not considered an option, partly due to the fact that many of the problems which have arisen over time could be traced directly back to the design of the communal access system – in each building the 176 dwellings shared just two lifts and one entrance. Over half a century, residents had appropriated the neighbourhood as best they could, but the estate's abstraction and scale made meaningful interaction between the public spaces and buildings impossible.

Two of the buildings were redeveloped as accommodation for the elderly with the addition of a medical centre at the ground floor. New homes were also added to their bases, deviating from the strict dimensions of the original blocks and employing earth red bricks in contrast to the abstract use of concrete above.

Two further blocks were redeveloped within the so-called "customer choice" concept, a Dutch scheme similar to that of the UK's Right to Buy scheme but with tighter controls on occupation and sale. This means that the socio-economic diversity of the residents will be greater, along with the existing ethnic diversity among the occupants across the blocks. For this tenure model, the scale of the buildings was an issue, so the architectural intervention was to break them down into three smaller

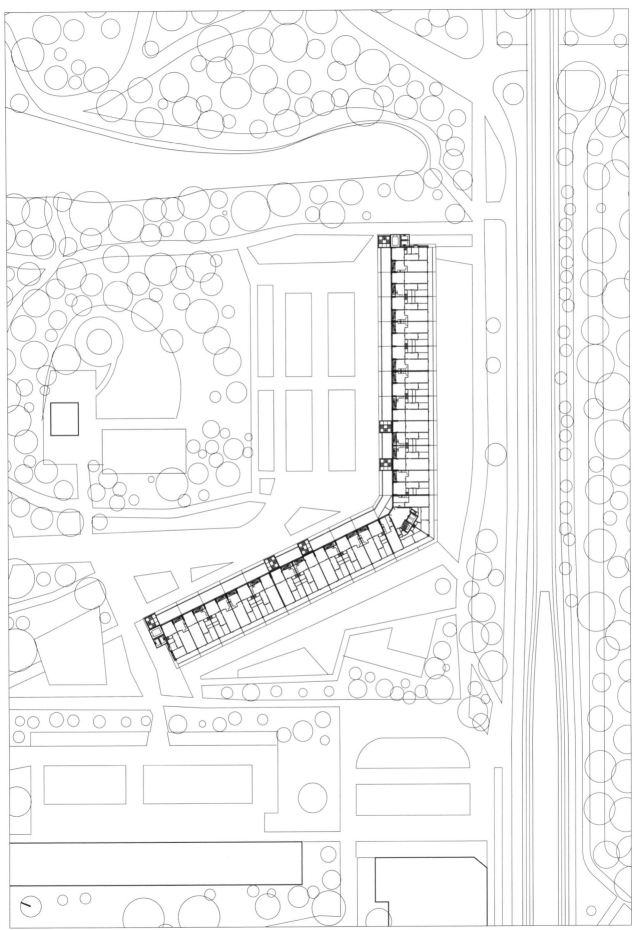

2.3.1 Ground-floor plan scale 1:1000

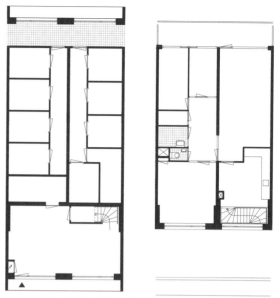

2.3.2 Maisonette plan after modification, scale 1:200

autonomously functioning segments, each having its own access system. The existing gallery and balcony were broken up through the removal of parts of the precast concrete deck, resulting in short and clearly arranged gallery-access decks.

biq's intervention is the result of a 10-year process to implement careful organisational changes to the blocks, avoiding unnecessary cosmetic changes in favour of meaningful, long-term alterations to adapt the blocks to a contemporary way of living.

2.3.3 View following addition of access cores and ground-floor amendments

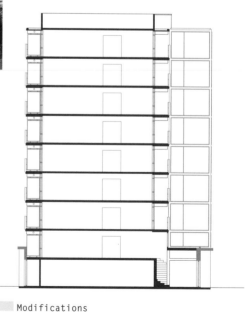

▓ Modifications
2.3.4 Section after modification 1:200

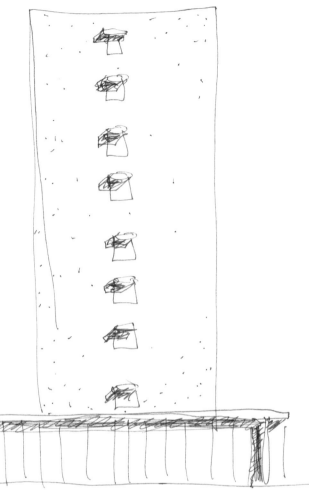

2.3.5 View of revised ground floor

2.3.6 Sketch of ground-floor amendments

2.3.8 Detail of concrete frame addition

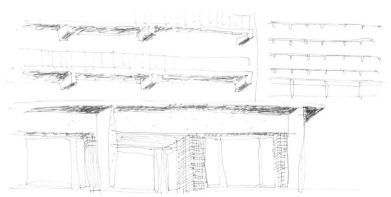

2.3.7 Sketch of ground-floor amendments

2.4
Hillington Square, UK
Mae

Country	UK
Location	King's Lynn, Norfolk
Client	Freebridge Community Housing
Cost	£30m, Phase 1 £4.9m
Funding	Local authority and Freebridge Community Housing funded
Units	319
Scale	5 storeys
Density	72 d/h
Mixed uses	Community café and masterplan includes new health centre
Tenures	261 affordable rented, 58 private leaseholder
Key dates	Start on site April 2013, Phase 1 completion November 2014
Procurement	Design and build with tender at Stage 4A equivalent

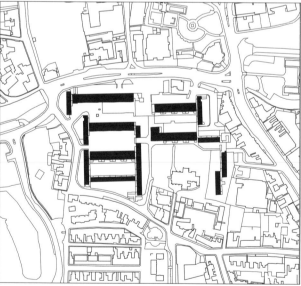

2.4.0 Location plan, scale 1:5000

The UK has been somewhat slow to incorporate the European method of sensitively reusing existing housing stock. The £30m refurbishment of Hillington Square in Norfolk is one of the few completed British examples of this attitude put into practice. The original slab blocks were completed in 1971, a development which differed dramatically from its architectural context and became associated locally with antisocial behaviour and an inherent absence of community (Figure 2.44). Given that the blocks have no protection in terms of architectural heritage, the estate was considered ripe for demolition and rebuilding. Following a transfer of the local council's housing stock to the non-profit housing provider Freebridge Community Housing in 2006, Freebridge was faced with the task of improving the standard of its housing stock and thereby the quality of life for its tenants.

If demolition had been the chosen approach, it is likely that the site would now be standing empty, as there was not sufficient funding for a complete new-build project. Instead, Mae proposed the refurbishment of 320 properties, remodelling of the estate layout and public realm improvements across 15 residential buildings. These are comprised of four- and five-storey buildings with communal stairs, lifts and deck areas.

The architects identified a series of design problems which they sought to resolve in the process of the regeneration of the estate, including long-access decks, low-grade outdoor spaces with no areas to play or socialise, ground floors occupied by garage doors and a low performing façade construction, making the homes expensive to heat. The design team reduced the size of the access decks, converting them where possible into balconies, and increased the number of stairwells in order to encourage chance encounters among residents. This design move was also aimed at promoting a sense of ownership among residents and a greater feeling of control over their immediate surroundings.

Regeneration projects such as these are as much, if not more so, an issue of sensitive resident communication as they are of architectural design. Credit for this scheme not only goes to the architects, but also to the housing association in investing time and money to understand the

2.4.1 Ground-floor plan, scale 1:1000

physical and social issues at hand and the effect these have on residents. For example, the government's behavioural insights team was commissioned to assess the concerns of the residents and what might be done to remedy ongoing social divisions within the community. While the interviews conducted by the team with residents gave the impression of a dangerous, high-crime environment, more detailed conversations with the local police identified crime levels to be on a par with the rest of the town and decreasing year on year. Security of tenure, employment status and duration of stay on the estate were all considerations, along with the physical implementations at a design level. The conclusion was made that, among other solutions, introducing new tenure types would produce a wider mix on the estate in order to combat some of the existing site-wide issues of high unemployment.

The project also raises the issue of the rebranding of estates and their desirability among the wider public. Consensus among residents was reached for the estate not to be renamed following the redevelopment, but to encourage each block to carry its own identity and be named individually. The stigma associated with such estates is one of the reasons why demolition is often the most obvious solution as a clear break from the past. However, the decision to examine in detail the social issues and to work with the existing fabric in an intelligent and pragmatic way, highlights a new way for UK local authorities to deal with housing stock they already control.

The first step was to remove the elevated access galleries that provided confusing access routes, formed a visual barrier and segregated the estate from its surroundings. More frequent and secure access cores were then added, providing more focused communal spaces with fewer users. Internally, bathrooms and kitchens were updated, windows replaced and new balconies were added above the new entrances. The number of ground-floor garages has been reduced, which enabled bedsit flats to be extended and new communal entrances to be accommodated.

The architects have successfully renewed the built fabric and have created a better definition of the public realm, whilst retaining the estate's sense of community and

2.4.2 Hillington Square (completed 1971)

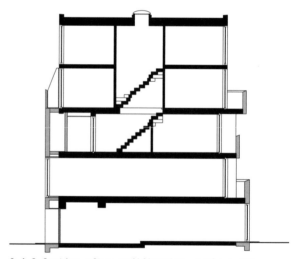

2.4.3 Section after modification, scale 1:250

finding value in its original architectural ideas. In certain circumstances demolition is the most appropriate solution to estate regeneration. However, this project is an example of architects working closely with a housing association to deliver within the social framework of estate regeneration, while creating an architecture with integrity and generosity.

2.4.4 New panelling and brown brick bays
define the entrances

2.4.5 Ground-floor garages removed, new
entrance bays provide a balcony
for the dwellings above

2.4.6 Third-floor deck-access divided
into private balconies

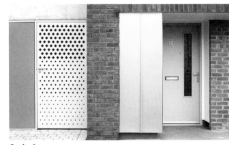

2.4.4

2.4.5

2.4.6

3.1
Granby Four Streets, UK
Assemble

3.2
Wohnprojekt Wien, Austria
Einszueins

3.3
K1 Co-housing, UK
Mole Architects

3.4
BIGYard, Germany
Zanderroth Architekten

New processes among residents

3

Introduction

The role of people in the design and delivery of social housing has never been more crucial or had so much potential. In the past, the architect as public servant commanded almost unwavering authority for the design of housing, a top-down approach was simply the normative way of doing things and residents were all too often passive recipients. However, big changes in policy and public opinion made the delivery of housing far more complex. The Town Planning Act of 1968 in the UK made "public participation" a vital inclusion in the design process, challenging the pristine ideals of modernism and paving the way for community-led approaches. At this time, across Europe radical movements concerning participatory processes in all areas of society were initiated and new ideas for collective living models came into sharp focus in the social democracies of northern Europe, which rejected both public authority and market inertia.

Since this time, consultative processes with resident groups have become a norm of design, informing outcomes in social housing schemes of all scales. However, with the failure of the private housing market and the limitations of local and central government bodies to take appropriate action, a new tendency towards alternative "active" forms of delivery where residents exercise control of their own fate entirely, has emerged. Models such as co-housing and housing co-operatives demonstrate different ways of building. Although commonly resulting in private or co-operative dwellings, they are included here as social housing, as they sit outside of the market and are not created by a "for profit" motive. These are houses for and by people, creating opportunities for citizens to shape their own city that can often result in high-quality architectural solutions and wider neighbourhood benefits.

Drawn from across Europe, the schemes in this chapter demonstrate the flexibility and particularity of co-housing and co-operative models. In contrast to market or public sector building where volume and repetition are often key to achieving economies of scale, the schemes can be bespoke and are able to embrace small infill sites to stitch together urban fabric and adapt quickly to new ways of living. Promoting community, the schemes offer new forms of habitation with a focus on shared space and opportunities for social engagement. As well as creating a means for bringing together shared amenities, such as laundry or kitchen facilities or open space, it can also mean substantial project cost savings and, over time, assist in their long-term sustainability.

These projects also reflect the changing role of the architect. When residents become clients and a collective of like-minded activists come together, the architect becomes a community enabler, developing negotiation and collaboration skills essential for successful delivery, great architecture and liveable cities.

Despite a long history, this alternative sector in the UK remains small and is often viewed as niche or experimental. From securing finance to procuring an architect with the right skills and the time required to manage the process, taking on a project of this kind is not without risks. There is much to learn from countries such as Germany, and cities such as Berlin in particular, where co-operative housing forms a significant proportion of all homes and 11% of all city rental housing.[1]

For areas outside London where development conditions have led to stagnation, diversification into these models for those able and interested could usher in new much-needed activity. Within London, building a home from scratch remains significantly cheaper than buying a standard product from the currently overheated marketplace. ■■■■■

[1] www.stadtentwicklung.berlin.de

3.0.1

**The Narkomfin Building, Moscow,
by Moisei Ginzburg with Ignaty Milinis, 1930**
This radical modernist block was conceived as a
"social condenser" and was a prototype for communal
living. Designed shortly after the Russian Revolution
of 1917, it embraced constructivist and feminist
theories and new architectural form to propose a
radical kind of social living, freeing people from
their traditional family roles. A large slab block
contained 54 dwellings and was linked to another block
containing shared kitchens, creches and a laundry. The
block was originally intended to have been expanded to
incorporate a library and gymnasium.

3.0.2

**Isokon flats, Lawn Road, Hampstead, London,
by Wells Coates, 1934**
The first example of modernist communal living in
the UK, this building offered an alternative urban
lifestyle choice. Pitched at an upwardly mobile type
of resident, its 34 simple apartments were studio-
like with blended living and sleeping areas, minimal
furnishings, small bathrooms and kitchenettes. The
block encouraged social interaction by providing a
large shared kitchen, dining and laundry space. This
typology was popular for an inter-war middle-class
avant garde, but did not catch on elsewhere.

3.0.3

**Byker Wall, Newcastle-Upon-Tyne,
by Ralph Erskine, 1969-83**
Replacing a rundown area of Victorian terraces,
this multi-family housing development was one of
the first major examples of community architecture
in the UK. The architect oversaw development and
encouraged tenant cooperation and trust by opening
an office on site. An exemplar of participatory
practice, it avoids the modernist tendency
towards singular monoliths seen elsewhere and
is one of the most highly regarded post-war UK
council estates.

3.0.4

**Iroko Housing Co-operative, Lambeth, London,
by various 1984-2004**
This mixed-use housing development was the result of
an extraordinary seven-year campaign mounted by the
Coin Street action group - a group of local residents
that saw off plans for a large-scale commercial
development. The community purchased 13 acres of land
and developed their own vision for housing in the area
that consisted of a series of mutual co-operatives.
Completed over 20 - years in phases, the Coin Street
community now consists of more than 220 dwellings and
is still growing.

3.1
Granby Four Streets, UK
Assemble

Country	UK
Location	Toxteth, Liverpool
Client	Granby 4 Streets Community Land Trust (CLT)
Cost	Approx £800,000 (initial 10 homes)
Funding	A mixture of grants and loans
Units	10 completed
Scale	2 storey terraced houses
Tenures	5 for rent, 5 for sale
Key dates	2014-present
Procurement	Traditional

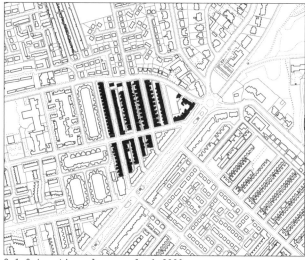

3.1.0 Location plan, scale 1:2000

The word "community" has become a loaded term when it comes to regeneration projects. It is often in the face of adversity or with a threat of upheaval that the potential for organisation and cooperation within a community comes to the fore.

Assemble's work at Granby in Liverpool demonstrates how architectural designers can assist a growing collection of CLTs across Britain in order to realise alternative forms of community housing provision. CLTs reflect an increasing tendency in communities to form small-scale groups with the capacity to organise and to initiate immediate change. Founded on the principles of community cooperation and the reinvestment of funds to avoid the potential for financial speculation, Assemble worked with local residents on a series of terraced houses in Granby in order to save, repair and renovate their homes.

The area of Granby was originally settled by merchants, artisans and shipping clerks, and since the 19th century it has been defined by waves of international migrant communities creating a rich social mix. Prince's Park in Toxteth was developed in the 19th century by Crystal Palace architect Joseph Paxton and the Welsh masterplanner Richard Owens, and is noted for its wide Victorian boulevards, villas, "brownstone" townhouses and brick terraces. Over time its reputation developed as a thriving cosmopolitan part of the city until misguided housing policies and socio-economic issues collided to initiate the decline of Granby. Liverpool's 1966 housing plan led to the demolition of three-quarters of inner city housing as part of a slum clearance programme. A similar process was then proposed in the early 2000s, when £2.2bn of public money was used as part of the government's Pathfinder scheme to buy up and bulldoze terraced properties all over the north of England with the aim of stimulating redevelopment that never materialised.

One such area was the terraced houses of Toxteth, which gradually fell into disrepair as they were primed for demolition. Local residents, of which only a small core remain, challenged the notion that total destruction and redevelopment was the only answer and continue to work tirelessly to invest their skills and effort in improving the Victorian streets. In early 2014, the Granby 4 Streets

3.1.1 Isometric site plan

3.1.2 Granby Street frontages

3.1.3 Neighbours in doorway

3.1.4 Wide-shot section of model

3.1.5 Model interior dining area shot

CLT took formal control of 10 homes from the council with the help of funding from Steinbeck Studio, a local investment organisation, and planned to renovate them into five homes for shared equity sale and five for affordable rent. In essence, it is an example of housing being provided on the basis of local need without the assistance of either the local authority or the private residential market.

The principle of CLTs is for the land to remain in ownership of the trust and then homes to be leased out to homeowners on long leases or rented at an affordable rate. The CLT fixes the price that homes should be sold at in the future, preventing exploitation and keeping homes genuinely affordable. CLTs are typically run by local residents and are therefore directly accountable for their own decisions, empowering tenants and owners with a sense of ownership over their immediate futures.

Alongside the redevelopment of properties are various ongoing sub-projects which include renovating retail units, using local labour through apprenticeships and organising street markets. The Four Corners project aims to bring four prominent corner shops back into use once the area becomes increasingly reinhabited, all funded through the mechanisms of the CLT. In addition, the Granby workshop acts as a small enterprise selling individual objects, including

pieces of furniture, fabrics and tiles in order to reinvest money back into the renovation works. Mantelpieces, for example, are cast on site, comprised of wasted brick and rubble, some of which have already been placed in newly renovated homes.

Assemble is a collective made up of around 16 members, a combination of young artists and designers who proclaim to "address the typical disconnection between the public and the process by which places are made". Working initially on temporary projects on in-between sites, it is now established as a hands-on design office which seeks to use inexpensive and flexible materials to suit a public-facing set of projects.

Straddling the line between art, architecture and genuine ground-up community engagement, Assemble has managed to operate in a field which goes far beyond the traditional heading of social housing. Aside from their role as designers, the success of Granby Four Streets is as much a result of the organisation and belief of the CLT, which will hopefully give other like-minded communities the impetus to act.

Transcript
Hazel Tilley
Granby Residents' Association and beyond

The Granby Residents' Association was very much a grassroots thing and it was in response to the council wanting to bulldoze the whole area and empty us out. It felt like social cleansing, and it felt like a punishment following the riots.

Anna Minter and Paul Ogoro pulled together the first public meeting. I went to the second one – I was encouraged on board by a woman called Dorothy Kuya. She was powerful and catalytic – she encouraged many people to believe in things which they never thought they could do. Dorothy had an interesting history and I learned a lot from her. I'm sorry that she died before the renovations started and that she never saw the streets and homes coming back to life. She was instrumental in stopping the total demolition of the Granby Triangle.

We started out trying to save the whole of the triangle and failed. When people refused to move out of their homes, it seemed to become a cult of abandonment by the city council. The street lights weren't fixed, the streets weren't cleaned, the bins weren't emptied, and the council took the lead off the roofs of the empty houses to stop it being stolen and didn't replace it. I think they thought: if we ignore the people who live in Granby, and keep chipping away, they'll give up.

And we were lied to. Councillors and council employees told us that the houses had to come down because they were sinking, because there was an underground river. They lied.

And then they said that nobody wanted the houses, so we phoned up the council to see how many people had applied for the houses, and they said: "oh, nobody can apply because we're not taking any names, so we've got no lists", so we put our own information out and got our own lists. The council would seem to listen to what we had to say, and then they'd just rubbish it. We talked to them about the Benwell project – houses for a pound. The Granby Residents' association was talking about ecologically sustainable buildings 20 years ago, and that too was pooh-poohed. We set up a working party with Granby residents and members of the council and wannabe developers, and the councillors that were involved were just using their phones under the table, texting, totally oblivious to what we were working towards.

We had a lot of this pretend consultation – they'd send people round and ask you what sort of house you'd like to live in and I'd say this one, in this area.

I remember one local councillor turning round and saying to me: "If it wasn't for people like you, we could have this area flattened and rebuilt by now." There was no trust of the residents. Councils, as much as they talk about devolving power, they can't possibly do that. You have all this talk about empowerment. Nobody's ever been empowered by anyone else because history tells you that you take power, because people with power don't give it to you, they don't give up their status. They didn't do it for black people, they didn't do it for women and they haven't done it for the people who live and want to live in Granby.

They wanted to knock down all of the bays on Cairns Street because they were "dangerous". It was demolition by stealth – they were starting to take away the features of the houses. So we stopped that. I was on my way to work and I got a phone call from Gina, a neighbour, saying: "Hazel, there's men come to knock down the bays, the bulldozer's coming," so I said: "get your van and block the street and phone up the *Echo*." I stopped on the motorway and phoned up the *Liverpool Post* and turned back home as fast as I could.

Five years ago or so I was actually thinking about selling the house and buying a houseboat. Empty houses either side, no central heating, no double glazing, I was heating the sky. There were no grants available because they wanted to demolish the place – so I was basically stuck with a disintegrating house, and I was just tired, it felt as though I was banging my head against a brick wall. We'd come up with so many ideas over the years about revitalising the area and bringing the houses back to use and they were falling down around us. You'd lie there in the night and hear a piece of wood go. ■■■■■

Transcript based on an article first published in the Granby Workshop Catalogue, edited by Assemble & Niamh Riordan, September 2015. With permission of Hazel Tilley.

3.2
Wohnprojekt Wien, Austria
Einszueins

Country	Austria
Location	Nordbahnhofgelände, Vienna
Client	Wohnprojekt Wien, SCHWARZATAL Gemeinnützige Wohnungs- & Siedlungsanlagen GmbH
Cost	€6.5m
Funding	Subsidies (loan), credit, capital resources from the dwellers (corporate share)
Units	39
Scale	7 storeys
Mixed uses	350 sq m commercial space, 700 sq m community space
Tenures	100% collective ownership by the association Wohnprojekt Wien
Key dates	2010-2013

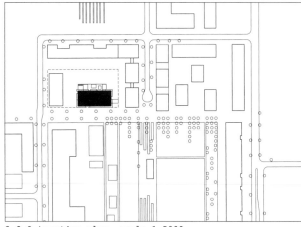

3.2.0 Location plan, scale 1:5000

Vienna has a long history of government-driven innovation in social housing as part of its strong tradition of welfare provision. Even today, Austria's biggest landlord remains the City of Vienna, which owns around 220,000 rental apartments while 60% of all Vienna households are subsidised apartments. Throughout its post-war history, Austria has been particularly resistant to market forces, resulting in a stable housing market. Housing co-operatives form part of this history and the Einszueins' project in Vienna continues these themes in a contemporary context.

Einszueins worked closely with the Wohnprojekt Wien housing group in the newly masterplanned area of Nordbahnhofgelände to create 39 co-housing units which accommodate a wide mix of generations, languages and cultures, including 67 adults and 25 children in a single building. The project is funded through a complex system of membership and "asset pooling", which aims to keep the cost of housing permanently low. This model requires residents to commit to long-term investment and to engage proactively in the financial management of the building, as well as to maintain a 10% liquidity fund for maintenance of the building. This comparatively large co-housing organisation has an advantage of being able to retain a funding structure which smaller groups do not always have the capacity to pursue.

The main emphasis of the project is the will of a self-organised community with the common aim to live together in the city in a sustainable, collaborative and open-minded way. The group describe themselves as "sociocratically organised", meaning that decisions are not based on a vote system but on the entire group openly discussing issues until a unanimous verdict is reached.

This attitude is mirrored by that of the architects' proposals to maintain a level of simplicity in the structure to allow for user specification. Unit sizes range from 35 sq m studios to 150 sq m shared apartments. Generous community and commercial space is managed by residents, allowing facilities such as a bike repair workshop and communal kitchens to create a lively and activated ground floor. Electric vehicles are used for residents to share trips, while a weekly market is organised

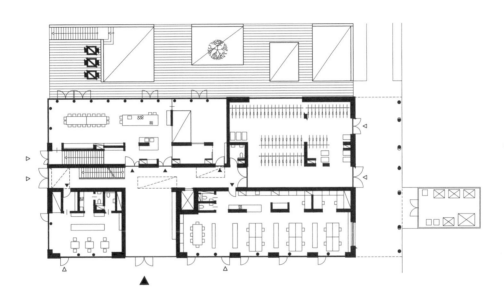

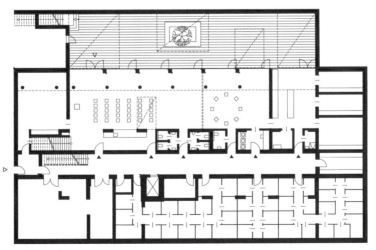

3.2.1 Floor plans, scale 1:500

3.2.2 Communal kitchen and dining space

on the forecourt and vegetable gardens form part of the communal property.

The design strategy was initiated from the outset as a participatory process for the planning of the communal spaces and individual apartment units. This continued with the car sharing, a communal garden for the neighbourhood, and ends with the common ownership of the building, resulting in active participation during all stages of the project´s development.

One of the fundamental aims of the project was to achieve a high level of individualisation inside the building envelope and to express this in terms of architectural design. For example, the void which runs alongside the main staircase facilitates spontaneous communication between residents, while the individual apartment units can act as spaces for retreat.

Some of the common spaces are located on the top floor, including a sauna, library and guest rooms, whereas on the lower floors there is a communal kitchen, workshops and event rooms, including a playroom for children and adults. The community also contributes to a fund which allows two housing units to be used to accommodate people particularly in need of social care in the local community. The ground floor commercial space is occupied by a small grocery store which provides locally sourced produce to the community, as well as hosting weekly performances and exhibitions.

The notion of sustainability within the built environment is one which is often misused as a term for a developer's sales pitch or merely a blanket requirement placed on all new developments. However, in this model of co-housing the term signifies a different meaning, specifically as a deliberate choice to live in a restrained and co-operative way.

3.2.3 Section, scale 1:500

3.2.4 Lower-level courtyard

3.2.5 Communal multi-functional space

3.3
K1 Co-housing, UK
Mole Architects

Country	UK
Location	Orchard Park, Cambridge
Client	TOWNhus
Cost	£8m
Funding	Private funding
Units	42
Scale	2-3 storeys
Density	48 d/ha
Tenures	100% private co-housing
Key dates	Completion scheduled for January 2018
Procurement	Design and build

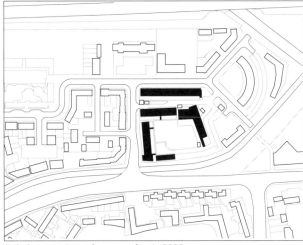

3.3.0 Location plan, scale 1:5000

Typical concerns for potential co-housing residents include compromised privacy and limitations on controlling the design specifics of their home. However, the custom-build sector is quietly growing momentum as policy begins to reflect the untapped demand for individual customisation of homes, in contrast to the existing constraints of the volume housebuilder model.

The K1 site in Orchard Park combines the ideas of co-housing the first such development in Cambridge, with the choice offered by custom-build. Cambridge City Council, along with Cambridge Cohousing Ltd (CCL), selected a developer to deliver 42 units on a site on the northern edge of the city. Having the council as part of the development team helped overcome a typical barrier to the co-housing model, namely the issue of high land values and a scarcity of plots. Selling off the land to the developer freed up funds for the council to invest in other parts of the city. On completion of the development when all the homes are sold, ownership of the land and the other shared assets will be transferred from the developer to CCL.

As a model, co-housing has the flexibility to allow for private ownership with the additional benefit of shared facilities which allow, rather than impose, residents to pool resources. Through sensible design, cars are avoided in the shared central garden and terraced houses have strong street frontages. Given that there is an element of individualisation in the resolution of the unit types in terms of layout and materials, this creates the potential for a much wider mix of residents, including families, young couples and elderly people looking to downsize from existing properties.

Designed by Mole Architects, the scheme provides four main dwelling types, which give purchasers various options depending on their specific needs. Using a low-cost timber construction system, the unit types offer a variety of different sizes, layouts and finishing options.

By devising a standard unit depth of 7.8 metres, building types A, B and C are all formed as terraced typologies which can be interchanged and positioned in different sequences as per the residents' wishes. Floor plans, interior design, number of bedrooms and external finishes are all decided according to the will and budget

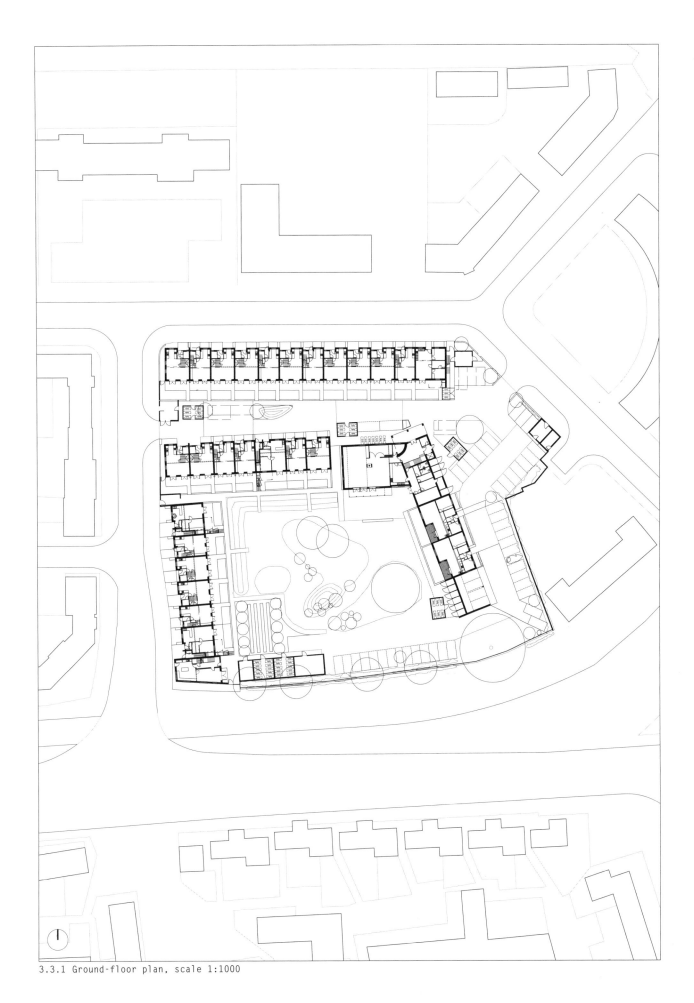

3.3.1 Ground-floor plan, scale 1:1000

3.3.2 Example of one flat, scale 1:200

3.3.3 Proposed view of communal garden

3.3.4 Proposed view of flexible communal room

of the user, a clear departure from the way UK housing is conventionally delivered. The presence of choice in the options available to residents offers an interesting dynamic with regard to challenging the often sterile nature of repetition in much of the UK's housing, and raises the standards of what is acceptable to prospective buyers. The homes are made available first to members of the CCL group who purchase directly from the developers and the properties are then leased on long-term agreements along with a share of the freehold.

Councillor George Owers of Cambridge City Council said: "There is a growing expectation on councils to enable and support custom-build and co-housing groups, so it's fantastic that Cambridge City Council is using such innovative methods to deliver housing by facilitating this development. The council is looking at a number of models for new housing provision and a mixture is needed to tackle the housing crisis."

Co-housing requires considerable time and resources from future residents in order to realise a project, but the long-term benefits for residents include improved customisation in design, personalised communal spaces, security of tenure and the stability of an engaged community. With support of landowning local authorities and enlightened developers, there is potential for co-housing to form a greater percentage of new housing in the UK as it does in mainland Europe. Whilst this example involves the sale of land and homes, the model, led by a local authority or housing association, could be used to provide an alternative model of social housing provision.

3.4
BIGYard, Germany
Zanderroth Architekten

Country	Germany
Location	Prenzlauer Berg, Berlin
Client	Bauherrengemeinschaft Zelterstraße 5-11
Cost	€15.5m
Funding	By the owners of the units
Units	45
Scale	4-7 storeys
Density	135 d/h
Tenures	100% collective ownership by the cooperative
Key dates	2007-2010
Procurement	Bespoke co-operative and architect-led construction company

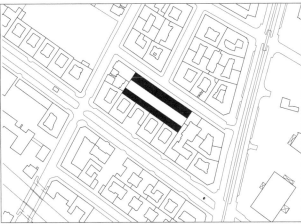

3.4.0 Location plan, scale 1:5000

The ideas which form many of today's *baugruppen* in Berlin can be traced back to the 1960s and 1970s when communes were particularly popular in the city. *Baugruppe* consist of like-minded individuals who form a co-operative or co-housing group specific to their requirements, whether young families, elderly people or those seeking to live in a particularly cohesive and sustainable manner. Around 10% of Berlin's new homes are built by self-build organisations, including *baugruppen* who claim to reduce the total build cost on housing developments by around 25%, by removing the developer and profit margins associated with the construction process.

Zanderrotharchitekten was employed as the architect practice for one such group on a problematic site in Prenzlauer Berg. This area, like much of the city, has undergone a substantial process of gentrification as housing stock has shifted into private hands in recent years. Typically defined as an area inhabited by the creative classes until the fall of the Berlin Wall, this part of former East Berlin is now highly desirable and becoming more expensive. However, change has been slowed by Berlin's long history of community-led development, rent controls and clear existing architectural language in terms of its perimeter blocks, which promotes a varied type of development.

On the quiet residential street of Zelterstrasse, the development was divided into three parallel stripes with 23 townhouses spaced generously across four storeys with a roof garden and face the street on one side and a large courtyard on the other. The townhouses are limited to four storeys in order to prevent overshadowing, while the other half of the site is occupied by 10 maisonettes with gardens and 12 penthouses above. The 1,300 sq m central garden forms the centre of the site with parking provided below ground. The garden is accessible to all ground-floor units and the scheme also includes a 250 sq m roof terrace with expansive views of Berlin, as well as cooking facilities, a sauna and four guest apartments.

The project was managed as a sophisticated joint building venture in which 45 parties – individuals, couples and families – joined to form a private company who took responsibility for the construction project under

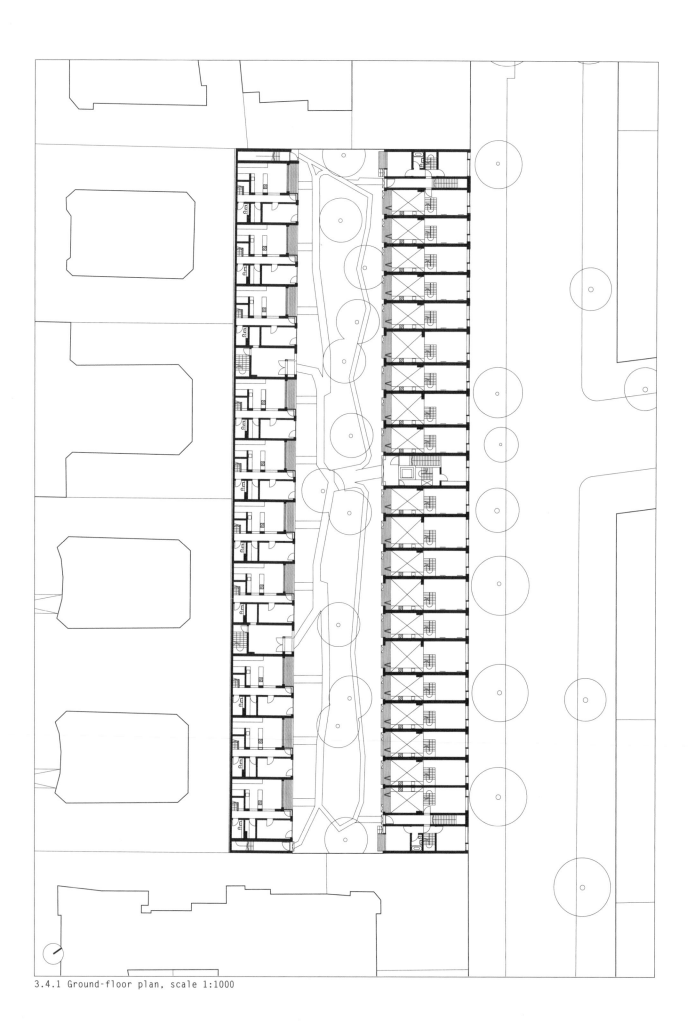

3.4.1 Ground-floor plan, scale 1:1000

3.4.3

3.4.2

the guidance of SmartHoming. This was a construction group instigated by the architects in order to cut out the developers and other consultants from the process, whereby zanderrotharchitekten provides both architectural and construction services. This maximises efficiency and value for money, in part by removing the various consultancy and their profit margins in typical building contracts.

The advantages of this method are increased individual freedom of design and high-quality architecture combined with lower costs. However, in contrast to other collectively funded projects, the architects limited the amount of input from residents on matters of massing, external finishes and construction methods, but room arrangements and internal specification were able to be customised. The nature of the long, narrow floor plans requires a 4.2-metre floor-to-ceiling height to allow sufficient natural light into the building. Free from the restrictions of standardised developer typologies, the BIGYard project allows individual internal layouts and an allowance for small intermediate spaces including terraces,

patios and the private courtyard, which may otherwise not have been considered economically valuable. Interestingly, there are no private gardens from the townhouses or maisonettes, with the only external space being a shared garden forming the central courtyard.

As opposed to the urban grain of the typical six-storey Berlin block around a tight courtyard, this scheme negotiates a leftover site by introducing a more horizontal emphasis to the street-facing façade. The grid-like concrete panel façade introduces a new composition to a homogenous district of the city as an expression of a different process of living, with an emphasis on a spirit of communal living.

The project shows an intelligent response to site, bespoke typological solutions, a coherent street edge and a generous arrangement of spaces on the courtyard side. While being born out of a movement which has a long tradition in Berlin, this project represents the potential for improved generosity and build quality of collective housing elsewhere.

3.4.4 View from upper-level maisonette bedroom towards townhouse

3.4.5 Townhouse plan, scale 1:500

3.4.6 View of communal courtyard

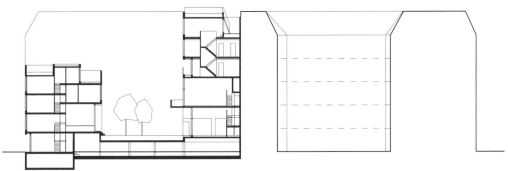

3.4.7 Section, scale 1:500

4.1
Osdorp mixed use centre and housing, The Netherlands
Mecanoo

4.2
Les Lilas young workers housing and crèche, France
Chartier Dalix Architectes + Avenier Cornejo Architectes

4.3
Lourmel mixed use housing, France
Trévelo & Viger-Kohler Architectes Urbanistes (TVK)

4.4
Carré Lumière, France
LAN architecture

Mixed
cities

4

Introduction

As economics and demographics shift, social housing and publicly funded projects are under pressure to deliver more than simple housing provision. Today, large cities such as London and Paris have ever more heterogeneous populations who live, work and play differently from previous generations. Accommodating flexibility and the possibility of further change is key to achieving long-term urban sustainability.

The strict, zonal planning definitions of the post-war city where residential, commercial and industrial uses were spatially segregated are becoming increasingly obsolete as land scarcity increases and the ways in which we inhabit our cities become once more intermingled. In many ways, the 21st-century city is echoing the mid-19th-century city, where the close proximity of uses were common and mixing was essential in an era before cheap and easy inter-urban travel and large-scale suburbanisation. At this time, typological hybrids emerged out of necessity and a shortage of space forced building owners to be efficient with land and creative in how they maximised a return on it.

Housing has long formed the majority of the built fabric of our cities and as such it must be part of an integrated urban strategy that is responsive to shifting social and economic patterns. Today, new working practices, modal shifts in transport and rising property prices in our cities are all encouraging an overlap between living and working spaces. These new spaces now demand access to a greater diversity of online and offline services and a range of social entertainments and distractions. At the same time, the ageing population profile of many European cities suggests more people living and participating in society for longer, rather than simply moving on into retirement in the suburbs. The impact of this could mean more multigenerational housing that can accommodate greater family mixes, or neighbourhoods with a greater range of shared social services that could support independent living for longer.

Within these emerging conditions, the creation of desirable housing will depend on the development of new approaches towards mixing people, housing preferences, employment and services. It will require housing providers of all kinds to learn from historic urban precedents and to embrace new scales, massing and building types to ensure the viability, longevity and dynamism of communities and their evolving lifestyles. It may also mean introducing planning policy changes that encourage flexibility and a degree of future proofing. In Paris, for example, there exists robust regulation at a city scale that encourages new residential projects to mix uses – typically social infrastructure, office space or retail – by discouraging ground floor residential use. In a city like London, such legislative change could be transformative.

The projects in this chapter look at emerging approaches to mixing and mixed uses. While none of the case studies achieve the ambitious call for employment and production at the heart of our cities advocated for by Professor Mark Brearley in his interview, they explore how architecture can accommodate a hierarchy and variety of uses. Whilst there is a housing crisis, there is also a crisis of space for work and particularly for fabrication and making in many of our cities. As densities increase and restrictions on building on greenfield sites remain in the UK, policy must adapt and architects must develop more sophisticated and hardworking typologies that use more intelligently the limited land available. ▬▬▬

Historic precedents

4.0.1

Tenement Street, New York, 1860s-80s
In the 19th century, huge population growth led to the
creation of tenements, which through regulatory reforms
assumed a common look and layout that came to define
the strict gridded streets of Manhattan and other
areas. At ground floor, tenement blocks incorporated
many commercial uses responsive to neighbourhood
need and in doing so created the city's celebrated
active and dynamic streetscapes, captured in art,
film and music.

4.0.2

Karl Marx-Hof, Vienna,
by Karl Ehn for the City of Vienna, 1927-30
This vast municipal housing scheme, housing 1,382
apartments, is a monument to a progressive period
in the city's housing history, commonly referred to
as Red Vienna. Aimed at workers, this high-density
distinctly urban inner-city scheme comprised large
articulated blocks with great archways providing access
to enclosed parkland, amenity space, schools, baths, a
library and a health centre for residents.

4.0.3

Stevenage New Town Centre,
by Stevenage Development Corporation,
led by Leonard Vincent, 1957
Designated in 1946, the commercial heart of this new
town featured the first pedestrian-only shopping area
in the UK. Influenced by examples in the USA, and in
particular Lijnbaan, Rotterdam, it was aimed to not
only provide retail space but also provide a modernist
setting for new urban living, with many blocks designed
to incorporate a wide range of flats and maisonettes
above, deemed essential for encouraging life and
activity at the town's heart beyond shopping.

4.0.4

Brunswick Estate, Bloomsbury, London,
by Patrick Hodgkinson, 1972
This mixed-use, low-rise, high-density scheme of 560
flats housing 1,600 people was designed to relate to
the types of housing and shops found at the very centre
of London. Situated in a predominantly Victorian part
of the city, it was a radical modern scheme with one-
and two-bed flats arranged in terraces that step back
and up from a central public space intended to be the
local heart of something much larger.

Interview
Professor Mark Brearley: An attitude about cities
Urbanist, London

It seems that in mainland Europe it is much more common to find technically refined and sometimes experimental combinations of residential and other uses within a single project or block. Would you agree that the UK struggles to achieve this and, if so, why do you think that is the case?

In my opinion, attitude about cities is where the issue lies; it is why the UK is spectacularly failing to address the overall challenge of making the kind of cities we want. The scarce examples that you do find of something approaching a sophisticated mix are rarely in combination with social housing; instead they are in places where the values are such as to create the desire to construct more varied accommodation. If you look at some of the market-led developments – particularly in London – it is actually impressive that there are such huge spaces on the lower levels that are non-residential. They could easily be carpet shops, factories, warehouses, schools, churches, all kinds of diverse activity, but of course they are not. They are only the uses from which the best rent can be won. However, the type built has the makings of exactly the sort of development some European examples are demonstrating.

We are not seeing good mixing within the revived forms of social housing currently being delivered in the UK. I find this shocking and I believe the origins of it are not primarily planning and economics – which of course play their parts – but attitude. It's just not seen as a key priority. The UK seems to have a particularly deep-rooted enthusiasm for early 20th-century ideas about "good city" that are based on neighbourhood and neighbourhood units. The disaggregated city is still seen as the warm-glow objective; to form little clusters where there is a congruence of locality and community, a domestic-focused place, while civic and city life is something that happens somewhere else.

Would you distinguish between the public attitude and the official decision-making process?

No. I think these ideas about "good city" have taken root in the public and official imaginations. It's a domestic-dominated mindset and it's anti-city. When local authorities get involved in housing development, their starting point is housing estates, and if they are imaginative and ambitious they say: "Let's build really nicely designed new housing estates." The mission is to create a piece of the city with a suburbanised economy, with its civic and economic life reduced to serving the population in the locality, hooked to the idea of neighbourhood that I think is ludicrous when applied to the wider city. Community is not congruent with locality, it is not as simple as that, and in reality I don't think any of us would want it to be that simple. As city dwellers we operate in many communities. Often these have a locational hook, such as where we live or where our children go to school, but we're also in lots of others. The idea that the ideal is to live in a locality that it is principally domestic is deep-seated and problematic. It comes from early 20th-century thinking, from the garden city movements and from ideas developed by people like Clarence Perry, who were working out how to overcome the problems caused by increased car use.

If we are responding to something as deep-seated as mindset, what role do we have as designers? Is it our responsibility to help to challenge those attitudes?

Yes it is, completely. Architects work for clients, so it's complex. But there are always opportunities to test limits, push boundaries and experiment, and it feels like now is the time when architects have a very significant role to play, especially in a city like London that is growing so fast and has such accommodation challenges. Architects have a crucial role in inventing ways of building the city, and people who are in positions to push forward development – developers, in their many guises and types – need architects to invent.

One of the recent forms of invention that went almost unnoticed was building housing on top of large supermarkets. When it was first proposed it was considered to be a ridiculous idea due to the challenges of flexibility, deliveries, noise and the need for uncompromised plans. However, as the economics started to shift, those developments started happening, resolving all the matters that had never been resolved before. That's a good example of invention such as needs to happen. Somebody has to lead the way. If you design a very successful development that incorporates mix in a way that people haven't dared to do before, then more people will follow.

Many architects working today are able to identify lots of spaces that they believe are particularly suitable for other uses, whether those are studios for artists, workshop spaces, creches, community spaces and so on. But at some point the financial modelling is run and it becomes very difficult to make the idea compelling. How do we challenge the dominance of economics in these conversations?

This is where planning should come in. We have to accept that cities are not as simple as grocery shops. They are not neat expressions of a market operating. They are supremely complex and very slow-moving beasts. Of course they operate in all kinds of markets, and there is a flexibility and nimbleness, but there are also factors that slow change.

For example, over centuries people have acquired and built for a long legacy schools, hospitals, churches and parks, with the intention of them being there forever. And then the public sector intervenes, on our behalf, by expropriating development rights and only handing them back when they believe it's appropriate. That is a huge interjection that we all buy into. Housing construction is also massively subsidised through tax incentives, direct grants and other mechanisms. There is an unshakeable consensus that we will find the money to build schools and healthcare. We all fret about whether as a society we can afford it, but the reality is that the funds are always found. There is short-term scarcity of things such as schools in a rapidly growing city like London, but there is never a long-term shortage. They always get built, always get paid for, and that's another hefty intervention in the market.

It is necessary to accept that the city is not a simple market. It is full of complex collaborative interventions and planning is a key one that is crucial to steering the whole evolution. We don't blink at the idea that we give playing fields nil land value, but it's a powerful intervention that

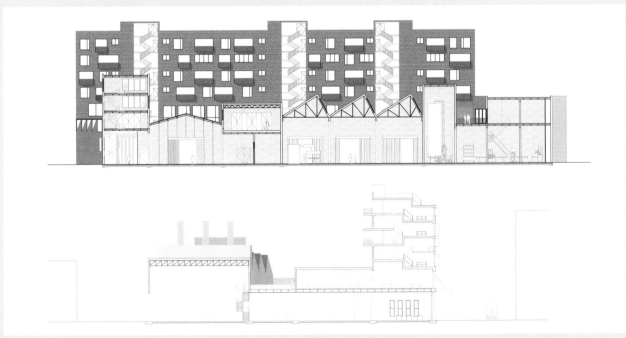

4.0.5 Student project study exploring combination of industry and housing

causes this. You could say: "Why should some people get space in the city to play football? They only do it once a week, why can't they commute to the edge of the city?" But we all support it. We designate the land as a green space and make it worthless for building on. The same has to keep happening with development generally. We need to start to push harder to hold onto urban diversity.

If we want to create mixed accommodation, then planning needs to say, on our behalf: "Actually, it's important to us that there's no residential below 10 metres around here, or below 4 metres there, because we need space for other uses." That's how some areas of post-war reconstruction in Rotterdam work. There is no residential coming to the ground, the staircases come down to the street, bins, bike stores and so on, but not the dwellings, and then there are the *hof* (we would call them mews or yards) that go through each block and serve all the non-residential activities such as shops, hospitality, workshops, storage and civic activities. The successful outcome is what happens when somebody says: "Now hear this, there is a principle and we should follow it." That's what planning needs to do.

You have previously referred to the need for planning regulation to be tightened in places and relaxed in others. What do you mean by that?

I am sure that planning needs to be tightened in its core mission, which is intervening in the land and property market in order to make sure that there is space retained and developed for the fully mixed city that we want and need. At one time, some decades ago, the threat seemed to be from commercial development wiping out residential with office blocks landing in your neighbourhood. Now it is residential that has become the strongest player in the market across large parts of London. We need to manage the consequences. But, on the other hand, we seem to be far too restrictive in the fine-grained parts of planning. One of the origins of the modern planning system was the protection of the residential amenity to satisfy those people with the loudest voices, the more eloquent or more prosperous. That has developed to the extent that now its OK to fill half of a dwelling's garden with a building for domestic use

without getting planning permission, but try to turn it into a workshop for your business and you will have the whole planning system piling down on you. There is a bias in the planning system in favour of residential amenity.

Planning doesn't seem fully able to nurture and clarify consensus around what kind of city we want, nor to interject to influence the configuration of our economic and civic life to make sure that there are the right types and quantities to keep the city welcoming and accommodating to all. It needs to be vital. Many non-housing aspects of our city are now struggling to find space, and yet there is still a robustness to – even an obsession with – rules linked to suburban ideals. This stranglehold is starting to be something of a democratic issue also, because most of us get to vote where we live only with our residents' hats on. Therefore the priorities of the people who get elected are overly focused on residential amenity. What about the rest? What about the economy and the civic life of the city that does not get a proper voice?

Should businesses be able to vote then?

Perhaps they should. Maybe democracy needs to be more nuanced. There are many things done by local authorities and one of the most important is planning, so why is it only residents that get to vote for the people that make planning decisions? Why is voting set up in such a way that this has to be their focus, so that the economy tends to be regarded as this naughty thing that happens "over there", necessary but somehow sordid?

Do you think that the role of mayors provides opportunities for cities to be viewed as wider organisations, whether in London or elsewhere?

Absolutely. I'm a great believer in elected mayors. It's a great idea that has been working very well in London and seems to have been effective also in the other cities that have adopted it. It allows for there to be a wider discussion about what the priorities are for our cities. It allows resource for exploring, testing and taking the initiative. It is successful at the strategic scale. I hope that in London there is a recognition from all mayors that not only do we have a housing supply crisis, but that we have more generally an accommodation crisis. This needs to be noticed and not allowed to be masked by the spectacular economic success of the city. There is sometimes a belief expressed that everything will be alright as long as the city is growing, even when some parts of its life are being suffocated and having to migrate away. That's mad. It is reckless to be so cavalier even if you don't care about social issues. If you do care about social issues then it becomes even more critical. We are developing an hourglass labour market with a burgeoning top and bottom tier, while the middle is shrinking. That's what's happening in London. It is a result of changes in the nature of the economy, but it is being magnified by the shortage of suitable non-residential accommodation, causing the city to lose some of its economic diversity.

A mayor can influence change by using the powers at their disposal to steer the nature of development. That's what I hope for soon. There must be a recognition that we should not just focus on housing development, but that we must develop pieces of city. We must have a big focus on developing a lot of housing, but please, not *only* that.

You have a particular interest in industry in the city, at all scales. How much of a factor do you think it needs to play within the design or our cities?

Industry needs a strong role, but it can be hard to define. Industry is all the repair, recycling, waste handling, production, storage, distribution and the servicing. Those kinds of activities are very significant in any city and in London they have all returned to growth. Industry also includes manufacturing, even though it is still officially written off as in terminal decline. In fact, it is expanding again, thriving even. A large proportion of it focuses on "just-in-time" products, such as the pints of milk that come from dairies in places like Chadwell Heath, and the bread that comes from the big industrial bakeries as well as a rapidly increasing number of smaller artisanal bakeries.

London has a long manufacturing history, but it remains a surprise just how much niche manufacturing

activity has survived. Much of the small-scale production these days is new and is by people that don't have a connection with that history. At the moment there is an insatiable demand for learning to make ceramics, with huge demand for space that will suit start-up ceramicists. At some point, some of these people become more serious and want to become industrial-scale ceramics producers. This is how you might end up with another Royal Doulton, which once had its factory in Vauxhall, by the way. We have seen historic breweries in London shrink until we are down to just one, but meanwhile 50 start-up breweries appear and start expanding. Then suddenly a large company decides to enter the market and opens a big new brewery in Ponders End, Enfield. All of this vibrancy needs accommodating.

A lot of the enterprise is being driven by people who want to be in the city. I am convinced that it's a huge opportunity as well as an accommodation challenge. Much of London's current industry can thrive in mixed situations. There are whole worlds of basic repair, metal fabrication, joinery, bespoke furniture, printing, food production and catering, and courier facilities. Every city has these. They are completely normal and the way in which we house them is critical. We should not wish them away; rather we should embrace and make space for them.

There's so much guidance around housing today. Do you think that it is inevitable that this begins to drive the process?

I do and there's nil guidance around the rest. That should be a key priority for a mayor. What's the equivalent of our extensive housing guidance for types of commercial and civic space? What are the key things that give flexibility and richness? What are the plan depth challenges, access needs, height and rectangularity demands? In Rotterdam in the 1950s and 1960s, they were clearly very aware of the fact that the commercial uses needed deeper plans than the residential, so that's what they were building. They were effectively rebuilding the historic city, but in a way that worked with service and goods vehicles. There is huge scope for simple new guidance.

Which countries do you think are doing mixed use well?

The interest in these subjects is very live around the world, but we each have only patchy experience. My experience is of parts of Germany, the Netherlands and Belgium. I am impressed by how interested they are and by the sense of urgency. In Rotterdam they energetically seized on what we were doing in London on high streets and our interest in urban industry, and now those are big themes for them. There, the city government now has a rich understanding of high streets and they're busy acting. All that post-war fabric I mentioned, as well as older fabric, much of which was really struggling is now reviving. They're really pushing the idea of linear vitality and the need for greater mix and the reintroduction of smaller-scale industrial uses.

Do you think the state should provide for that framework or should it be more embryonic?

There's a lot of useful collective intervention that could be done and that should include a local government role in development. It's not useful for us to think in terms of a diagrammatic division between public and private. We should see the city as a collective project, one that we are all in together. The UK should stop having such communal angst about the distinction between public and private sectors. Other countries don't fret about that in the same way.

You have previously described London's current situation as a "fast de-mixing process". What do you think would be the end point if the current trends continue unabated, without any significant intervention through planning or other mechanisms?

One possible end point is a spectacularly dynamic and expanded centre with a 1,000 sq km housing estate around it: an increased density suburb that consists only of residential use plus the things that are locally required to support it. In such a nightmare scenario there would not be any significant large-scale economic and civic life going on outside the

centre. It would be a giant central business district plus a super-suburb. And lurking beneath the surface, maybe discreetly unmentioned at polite dinner parties, the fact that all the poorer people would have been pushed further away, commuting for hours in order to keep the city working, and the vans and lorries would be crawling in and out each day from way beyond the city boundaries. That's the grim version that nobody wants, but it could easily happen. To head it off we must activate the impressive consensus against it. We must all get busy! ▬▬▬

Throughout the 2000s, Professor Mark Brearley worked with the Mayor of London, developing urban strategies with the Architecture And Urbanism unit and then Design for London. Shaping regeneration projects and capital-wide initiatives, including the All London Green Grid, the Mayor's Great Spaces and the Outer London Fund, writing and teaching, he is an advocate for the potential of cities to enhance our quality of lives and promote diversity.

4.0.6 Axonometric sketch showing organisation of co-working, production facilities and making space at Meridian Works, Enfield London

4.0.7 View showing integration of Meridian Works within wider Meridian Water mixed-use masterplan led by the London Borough of Enfield

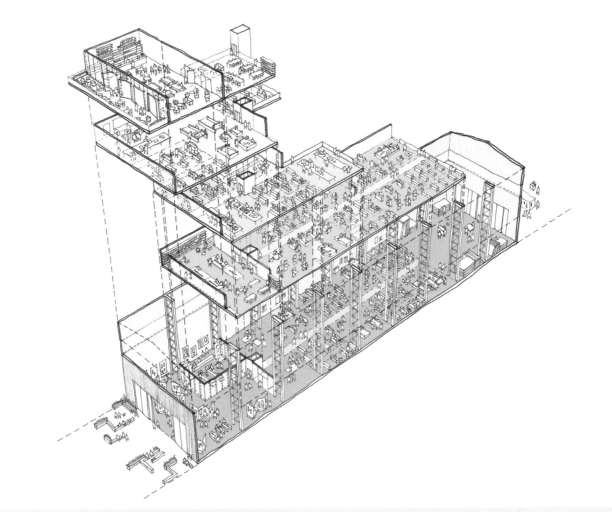

4.0.6

4.0.7

4.1
Osdorp mixed use centre and housing, The Netherlands
Mecanoo

Country	The Netherlands
Location	Osdorp, Amsterdam
Client	Ymere Ontwikkeling and Amsterdamse Stichting voor Katholiek Onderwijs
Cost	€15m
Units	51 apartments, 21 single-family homes
Scale	3-6 storeys
Mixed uses	Primary school, children's day-care centre, 3,500 sq m sports hall, healthcare centre
Tenures	100% Social housing
Key dates	2005-2011

4.1.0 Location plan, scale 1:2000

The Westelijke Tuinsteden or Western Garden Cities, were built on the periphery of Amsterdam in response to the housing shortage after the second world war, following modernist principles. The long process of renewal at Osdorp started in 1993, with a focus on two elements: the spatial framework and the building zones. The urban reconfiguration introduced new parks along previously underutilised open spaces and transformed the street hierarchy to create distinct neighbourhoods. The objectives of the architectural strategy were to diversify the typologies and tenures, whilst improving the relationships between public, communal and private areas.

The Reimerswaal neighbourhood consists of nine urban blocks and features broad streets and car-free squares; the regeneration project was a partnership between the city council and local housing corporations. Mecanoo designed the first plots, with a programme combining a school, sports hall, preschool playrooms, a children's day-care centre, a community centre, 51 apartments and 21 single-family homes. The urban block successfully combines social housing and educational spaces, and is the result of a collaboration between the developer, the school board and designers.

Community and social functions were placed at the ground floor and arranged so as to address the hierarchy of streets, with the school entrances, preschool playrooms, day-care centre and apartments located on the main route, and more informal residential façades with protruding balconies and semi-recessed windows on the side streets. The block successfully integrates the contrasting sized volumes and different housing typologies into a coherent building. It steps down from six storeys to three on the north, where it opens up to the green courtyard that is accessible to both students and residents. Above the school are four levels of apartments, and to the quieter northern street there is a line of terraced homes

The central courtyard is visible from the glazed school entrance, sharing light and activating the public realm, and a second school entrance is situated off the raised courtyard. The school façade was designed in collaboration with artist Elspeth Pikaar, who transposed texts and drawings of pupils onto glass panels that form

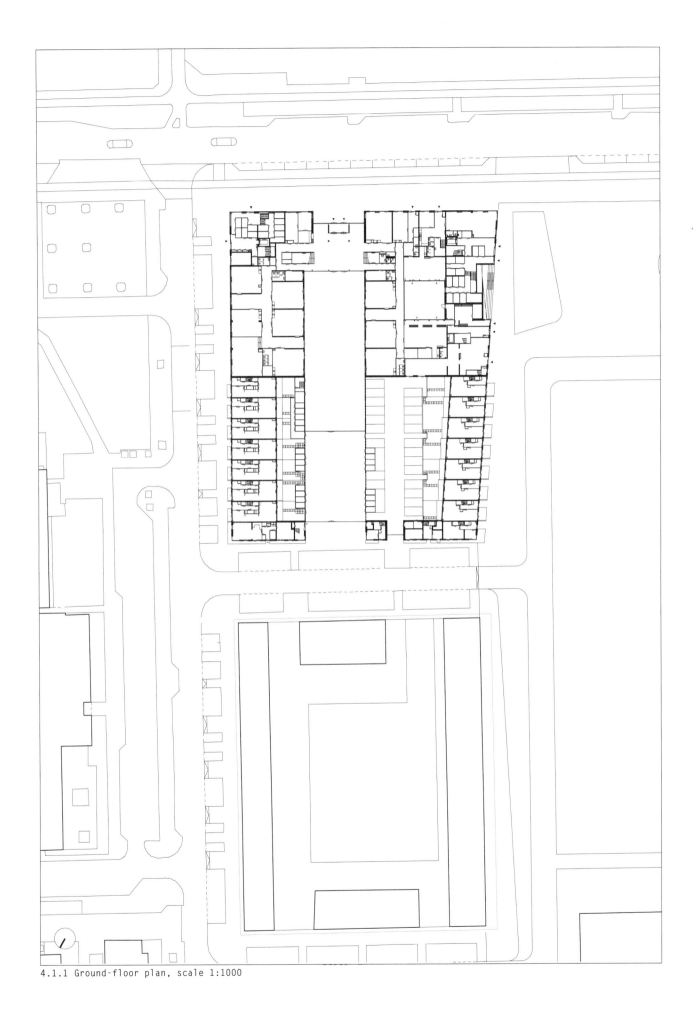

4.1.1 Ground-floor plan, scale 1:1000

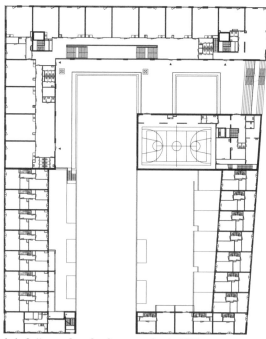

4.1.2 Upper-level plan, scale 1:1000

a ribbon around the building. The intention is to illustrate the progression through the study years at the school and enhance the pupils' sense of connection with their school and the neighbourhood. The interior of the school is meticulously child-friendly and a colourful palette has been used throughout.

An increasing common typological mix of school and homes, this project successfully resolves the various access and overlooking issues. It also accommodates the contrasting volumes into a coherent block that addresses the hierarchy of surrouding streets.

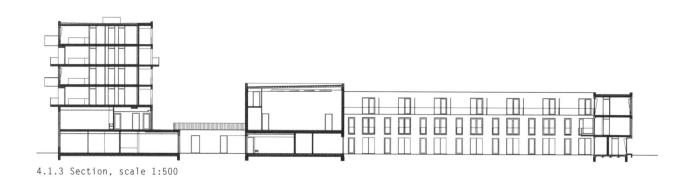

4.1.3 Section, scale 1:500

4.1.4 School and housing combined with raised courtyard

4.1.5 Housing accommodated above school

4.2
Les Lilas workers' housing and crèche, France
Chartier Dalix Architectes + Avenier Cornejo Architectes

Country	France
Location	Les Lilas, 20TH ARR. Paris
Client	Régie Immobilière de la Ville de Paris (RIVP)
Cost	€19.6m
Funding	Public
Units	240 studios for young workers and migrants and 66-space crèche
Scale	10 storeys
Mixed uses	Crèche
Tenures	100% social
Key dates	Competition November 2009, completion October 2013
Procurement	Local authority-led delivery appointing contractor and architect

4.2.0 Location plan, scale 1:5000

Built for the Paris public housing agency (RIVP), this project houses three core elements: a hostel for newly arrived immigrants, a hostel for young workers, and a 66-place day-care centre on the ground floor, as well as other supporting communal facilities. Located in Paris' 20th arrondissement, it is both Parisian and typical of the Les Lilas area with the building's unique location resulting in it playing an important role as a point of reconnection between the two areas. The building is located within a complex urban area that is undergoing immense change. Just to the west of the site, Paris' second ring road has been partially decked over and redeveloped to provide a new bus interchange, arthouse cinema and public open space. The building sits on a sloping site and responds to these elements, using them as new reference points.

The building is visible from the new neighbouring public spaces and despite its variety of uses, it presents itself as a homogenous masonry block with a series of clear articulations to the mass: two breaks – one vertical and one horizontal – and a series of setbacks at its top. The horizontal break in the façade at the third floor announces a common space for residents, from which they can access all the community uses. These include a media centre, sports hall and group kitchen, and the whole floor offers the residents of the two hostels the possibility of interaction as they participate in different activities. This was a critical response to the client's ambition to allow for the diverse groups of the two hostels to have the opportunity to meet and to socialise.

The vertical break provides natural light to the street-facing circulation and offers a glimpse into the life of the hostel from the street. On each floor it forms an additional space for informal meetings and conversations; architecturally, it creates a break within the necessarily repetitive and efficient distribution of flats, of which there are 30 on each of the typical floors.

The crèche is located entirely on the ground floor with a primarily south-facing aspect into the centre of the urban block; the rooms enjoying generous light and extending to the outside play areas. An aerial canopy made from a light metallic mesh covers the play areas, giving a sense of

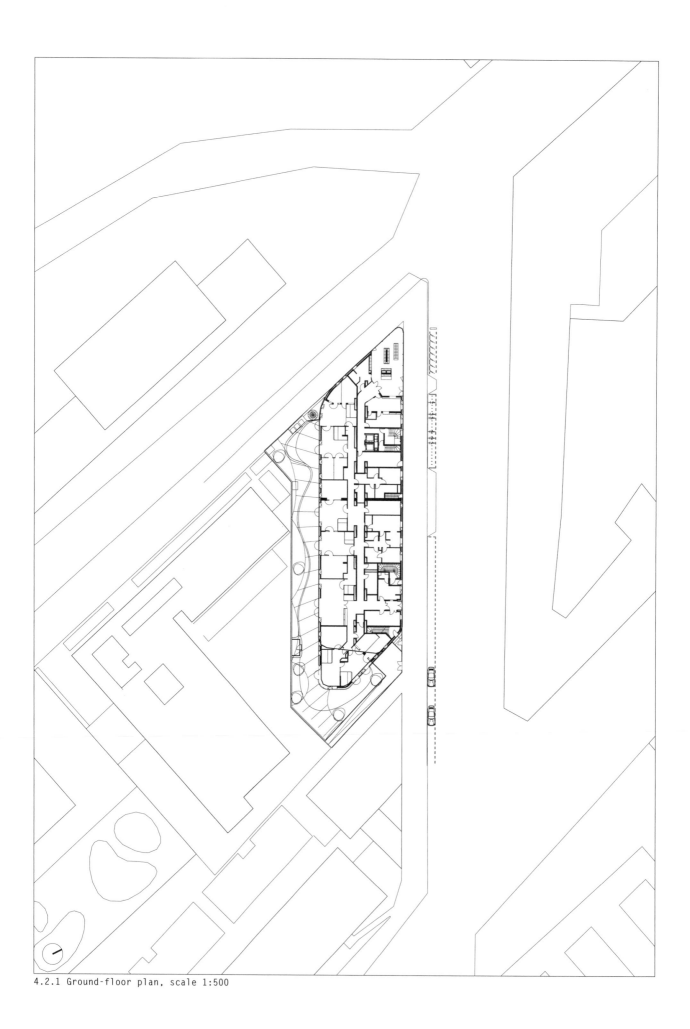

4.2.1 Ground-floor plan, scale 1:500

4.2.2 Unit plan, scale 1:200

4.2.3 Completed scheme from main square

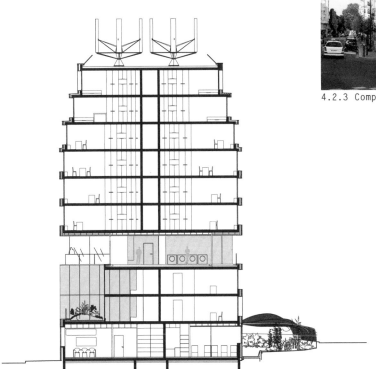

4.2.4 Section, scale 1:200

4.2.5 Vertical and horizontal
breaks announce common spaces

protection, but allowing sufficient light to penetrate to the centre of the building's plan.

Within the hostel, the typical flat type is designed to make maximum use of the space available and to provide a flexible living area. Shutters allow for the kitchenette to be separated from the living space, and the table contains built-in drawers. There are two sleeping options, either a pull-out bed or a trundle bed. A bench and wardrobe are also designed to maximise space and comfort, while the bathrooms are naturally lit using a light well.

Referencing the typical buildings around the outskirts of Paris, the choice of the façade materials is typical of the high quality demanded by the client RIVP. The building is faced in brick, which is durable and easy to maintain; the

bricks have been placed using a square-edged joint cut and are handmade. This semi-industrial manufacturing method gives the brick a varying texture in coal-like tones. The two cuts to the form of the block are clad in copper, the luminosity and reflective quality of the material contrasting with the velvet-like texture of the dark brick.

Part of a larger regeneration scheme addressing an important new crossroads, the building responds to the constrained and sloping site by occupying the entire ground floor with a robust architectural language. Accommodating an ambitious mixed social programme, the communal spaces are located on the fourth floor, celebrated as a break in the building's dominant massing and materiality, they form a prominent addition to the street and square.

4.3
Lourmel mixed-use housing, France
Trévelo & Viger-Kohler Architectes Urbanistes (TVK)

Country	France
Location	15TH ARR, Paris
Client	SemPariSeine
Cost	€24m
Funding	Public
Units	54 social housing,
	25 housing shelter
Scale	4-9 storeys
Mixed uses	101-room retirement home,
	a day centre, a crèche
Tenures	100% social housing
Key dates	Competition winner 2009,
	completed 2015
Procurement	Public competition for architects,
	construction management process
	during construction phases

4.3.0 Location plan, scale 1:5000

The project is located in the heart of Paris's 15th arrondissement, near to the banks of the river Seine. The site formerly belonged to France Télécom and was previously occupied by a disused factory. The large-scale urban blocks comprise large-scale modernist apartment buildings that dominate, giving the district its urban identity, but interspersed within the blocks are pockets of greenery that include tree-covered courtyards, small inner gardens and large planted terraces.

The project is an example of an ambitious mixing of uses that are accommodated in an ensemble of three buildings, each of which brings together two distinct programmes. There are 30 social-housing units and a large commercial unit in the first building, a women's shelter and 24 social-housing units in the second, and a retirement home with a day centre and a creche in the third. In composing these three buildings, the designers were interested in exploring the typological variations between uses and the ways in which they could be interwoven on a complex site. The final arrangement was developed through a thorough understanding of the requirement of each programme, its needs and their suitability for different sites within the block.

The compact, sculpted volumes of the corner building are visible from its four sides and act as a focal point that leads the visitor to the centre of the site. The building contains 30 social apartments and a shop at ground floor. The apartments are accommodated over the eight storeys above ground with a compact central core. The organisation of the plan exploits the corner site of the building, with halls leading to corner living rooms. The open kitchens are able to be separated by partitions, or to act as an extension of the volume of the living room.

A passageway acts as an entrance hall to the block and is sheltered by a cantilevered overhang from the building above. Due to the compact site and the requirement to achieve sufficient density, exterior spaces are placed at roof level in the form of a communal terrace that is accessible to all residents.

The women's shelter is housed in the north half on the ground and first floors, in two parallel buildings separated by a garden. This distinct and specialist use requires calm and protection, and is reached via a passageway that leads

4.3.1 Ground-floor plan, scale 1:1000

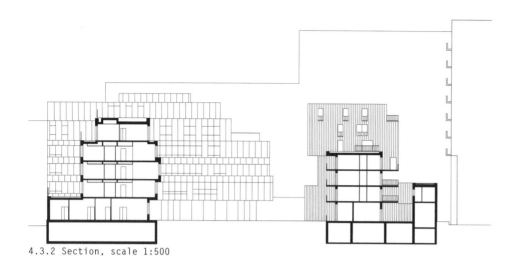

4.3.2 Section, scale 1:500

4.3.3 Street frontage with commercial space at ground

4.3.4 Women's shelter and social housing

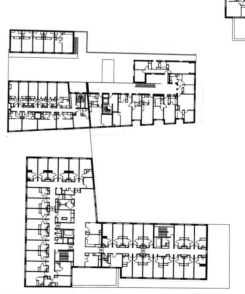

4.3.5 Unit plan, scale 1:1000

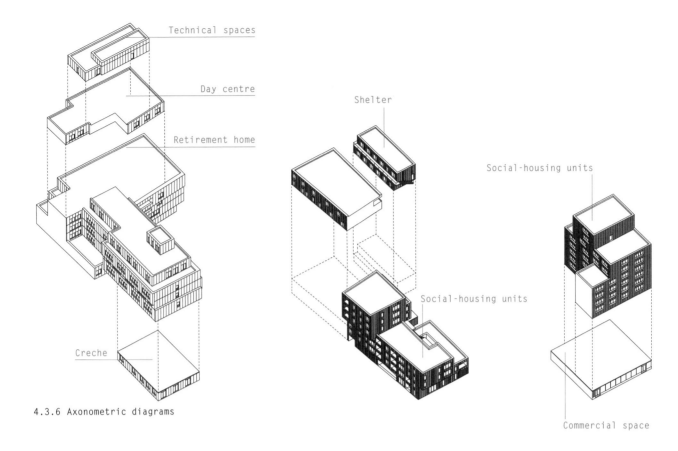

Technical spaces

Day centre

Retirement home

Creche

Shelter

Social-housing units

Social-housing units

Commercial space

4.3.6 Axonometric diagrams

from the north-east corner of the central square through to the inner garden. The ground floor contains the reception spaces, communal rooms, offices and nine living units. The living units are accessed on the ground floor via the garden, and on the first floor either by an interior circulation or an exterior passageway.

The social housing apartments are grouped in the south part of the building, accessed from two cores, an internal (with a staircase and a lift) that reaches the sixth floor, and an exterior staircase with passageway that leads to the third floor. Almost all the building's 24 apartments have an exterior space, and within those with three rooms or more, this is provided in the form of loggias. All units are provided with large, plate-glass windows that provide high levels of daylight and echo traditional Parisian workshop buildings. The ground-floor level includes the access ramp to the car park (for the entire complex), communal spaces and two apartments. The first-, second- and third-floor living units are organised around a central band with the wet rooms on either side. As a result, most of the apartments have more than one

aspect. The apartments on floors four to six are arranged around the central core; each floor being slightly different due to the successive staggering on the east elevation.

The large building to the west of the central square caters for two age groups – older people and children – and their specific needs. Composed of staggered horizontal bands, the façade is chamfered to address the central public square. The creche is an independent unit at the end of the ground floor. The rooms of the retirement home are on levels one, two and three, with offices, the day centre, communal spaces on the ground floor and apartments on the top two levels.

Together, the three buildings successfully interweave a complex set of briefs to exploit a challenging site that includes both block edge and interior. The project is an example of how a nuanced approach to building arrangement – in the form of the ensemble – provides the opportunity to successfully vertically stack a wide variety of uses, without compromising the daylight and privacy of communal spaces.

4.4
Carré Lumière, France
LAN architecture

Country	France
Location	Bègles
Client	Ataraxia
Cost	€8m
Units	79
Scale	3-6 storeys
Mixed uses	Commercial units (ground floor)
Tenures	Market-rate and publicly-assisted housing
Key dates	Competition 2009, built 2015
Procurement	Delivered by private investor

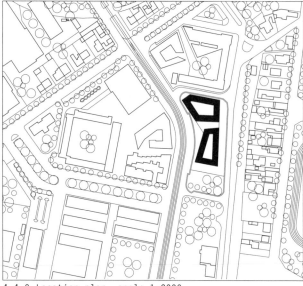

4.4.0 Location plan, scale 1:2000

The need to offer adaptability and flexibility in housing is of critical importance in helping to create strong communities; homes that can adapt to changing needs allow residents to remain even as their circumstances change. However, adaptability can often be at odds with a strong urban response, and combining a clear urban form – such as the courtyard block – with genuinely flexible dwellings is both spatially complex and economically challenging.

LAN was appointed to develop housing in the form of courtyard blocks and within an overall plan that aimed to clearly define a number of public spaces as part of an urban rehabilitation programme. The project is for 72 social housing apartments. The architects describe Bègles as one of the few communes in France where one can still carry out such a project. It is governed by the Green party, who they consider to be more open-minded towards new ideas for housing, and it is also an area that is being completely reconstructed following the demolition of a grand ensemble. An entire neighbourhood is being redesigned on new urban and architectural principles. The architects felt that being provided with such a tabula rasa required that the project had to address issues that were much larger and overarching than the locale itself.

As with many similar projects, the requirements for the project were highly complex and in combination verged on contradiction. The designers were required to build at high density and to make best use of the available land, but at the same time to give people of limited means the chance to live in a place of generosity and adaptability that could respond to their changing circumstances. They needed to envision building forms and housing typologies that could combine a desire for intimacy or privacy with the pleasure of socialising, but could also respond positively to both immediate and long-term environmental requirements, including the potential for significant climate change. Fundamentally, the architects identified cost as a potentially major constraint to combining all of the project's aims. In order to successfully resolve the scheme they felt that it would be critical to question the current models of housing production, in which high construction costs were driven by

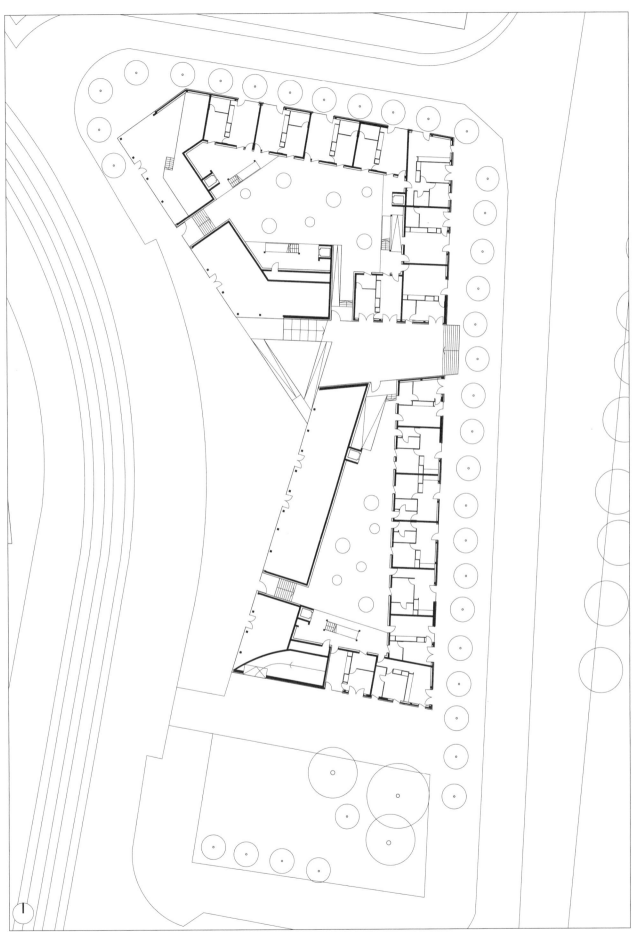

4.4.1 Ground-floor plan, scale 1:500

complex public procurement processes that risk transferring public benefit to excessive contractor profit.

Typologically, the project aims to develop housing that can act as a hybrid between the house and the apartment. The buildings are conceived as an envelope that can adapt in size, doubling their density if required to do so. Each apartment has access to a winter garden and the residents are able to use this to increase the size of their living area without the need to obtain building permits. In response to the potential growth of a family, residents are able to add a room to the home within the framework that has already been constructed, or to remove it once this space is no longer required. The adaptability of these spaces also provides climatic control for the individual resident, each home having the potential to use their exterior space as a windbreak, a mini-greenhouse or, conversely, as a means of cooling or ventilating the home

As in a freestanding house, each apartment has four façades, three of which are exposed. The architect's intention was for apartments to have the same qualities as a single-family home – such as sense of privacy, private external space and a strong sensory contact with the outdoors. The housing typology is based on the traditional worker's house in the Bordeaux region known as an *échoppe*. The principles of this typology are simple: habitable rooms are located off a side corridor that ultimately leads to a garden, traditionally located at the back of the dwelling.

The delivery of the project demonstrated the absurdity of the typical economics of housing construction; it attempted to provide homes to those who needed it with as few middlemen in the procurement process as possible. Bègles was built at a cost of 1,000€/sq m, far below the typical cost in the region, and at approximately twice the proportion of façade-to-floor area (typically a major cause of higher costs). This was achieved through rationalisation of building structure and services, prefabrication and strict management of budget during the development of the design. The initial costing was carried out factoring in only a minimal rate for the external loggias; this bespoke approach to the budget was appropriate to the careful strategy developed.

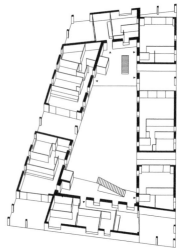

Typical floor layouts of the two blocks

4.4.2 Cut-away floor plans showing northern courtyard

The architect's ability to engage with the wide range of issues, perhaps most importantly challenging the typical market-led approach to costing and procurement, has delivered a scheme of innovative typologies and generosity of space and light.

4.4.3 Mixed use at ground and deeply recessed loggias to homes above

4.4.4 View across courtyard from private échoppe

Urban responses and challenging sites

5

Introduction

Great affordable housing, just like a new metro transport system or a park, is a key part of the social, economic and environmental sustainability of a city. When housing is successfully integrated into the wider urban fabric of a place, it can play a crucial role in creating opportunities for people and contributing to an enhanced quality of life.

In the early 20th century, industrial pollution, urban poverty and disease were all instrumental in the complete rethinking of our cities. Good housing, clean air, sanitation, open space and efficiency of movement became important objectives of post-war planning, which promoted comprehensive reconstruction, defined strictly controlled zones of residential and commercial uses and kept pace with the growth of car ownership with systems of new roadways and car parks.

Across the 1960s and 70s, this pattern of urban development became normative throughout Europe, but in accommodating the car and then seeking to create sanctuary from its adverse effects and in zoning out other uses, many housing estates inadvertently became detached from the idea and function of the city. Concurrently, experimental approaches to urban form, with their origins in the Modern movement, and advanced construction techniques often combined to create buildings and landscapes that lacked human scale and straightforward navigation.

By the late 20th century, this dispersed approach to urban organisation had caused fractures in the continuity of our cities and had left many people isolated from each other at a neighbourhood level, and at an urban scale had put them at a distance from the opportunities of city life. The replanning of Europe's cities pushed many people out to new estates at remote locations, perhaps most notably in Paris to the banlieue and the new towns in the UK. However, one does not need to be at the physical edge of a city to feel a sense of being peripheral to its life and activities. Housing developments of all kinds – social or private – that fail to connect areas, create physical barriers between neighbouring districts and display hostility to the urban grain of a locality, risk the creation of insular environments that can foster low aspirations, stoke resentment and fuel tensions.

Social housing requires the creation of places that are connected to the convenience and conviviality of cities. The case studies in this chapter represent the many ways in which new buildings and refurbishment can achieve this. Most fundamental among them are new housing interventions that seek to repair fractured districts and streets, open up through routes, articulate legible boundaries between public and private space, and reclaim the street as a space for social exchange. The next generation of social housing needs to summon the confidence of the post-war era and embrace the potential of urban sites of all kinds, rather than creating a wasteful *tabula rasa*. An example of this is the refurbishment and intelligent insertion of new units into existing estates on constrained or awkward sites, previously considered too difficult or troublesome for housing. To embrace the opportunities we may need to challenge the orthodoxy of certain building controls and planning guidance that make generalised assumptions about such factors as building close to railways, for example, or exceeding certain heights or densities.

The challenge of our current urban age can be summarised simply as one of increasing densities. While loaded with complexities, our cities are growing and need to find new ways to accommodate more people at the same time, maintaining liveable, sociable and human environments. Regardless of specific form, the projects in this chapter represent ways in which to tackle this through innovative building programme, intelligent phasing and layouts that preserve existing homes and plug new neighbourhoods into the greater urban whole. ▬▬

5.0.1

Bedford Square, London, 1775-80.
Laid out as part of a wave of residential speculation initiated by the great estates, this is a prime example of Georgian town planning at a grand urban scale. Following the typical development model of the time, the layouts were determined first by the ground landlord or, in this case, the Bedford Estate, and plots were leased to teams of private builders who developed housing according to covenants that determined their scale and massing.

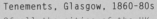

5.0.2

Tenements, Glasgow, 1860-80s
Of all the cities of the UK, Glasgow is unique for the popularity of apartment or flat living. In the 19th century, there was a boom in the construction of near-uniform streets and neighbourhoods of handsome brownstone tenements arranged around internal courtyards catering to all social backgrounds. While in the post-war years many poorer areas fell into decay, these are popular today for their generous proportions and robust construction.

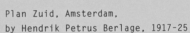

5.0.3

Plan Zuid, Amsterdam,
by Hendrik Petrus Berlage, 1917-25
The celebrated South Plan was a concerted effort by Amsterdam's municipal authority to manage the large-scale expansion of the city. Starting life as a dense picturesque scheme attached to old Amsterdam, the plan was redesigned for the spacious arrangement of large residential, mostly social blocks set out along broad new avenues. The area became synonymous with many projects of the so-called Amsterdam School.

5.0.4

Quartier du Grand Parc, Bordeaux,
by Jean Royer, 1959-75
Created by draining a vast wetland, the development is an ambitious urban extension where parkland and amenity space is central to the arrangement of large modernist residential blocks. Covering over 40ha, with 8ha of parkland, the quarter contains 4,000 social-housing units. In contrast to other developments of its kind in France, it has remained popular and part of the life of Bordeaux rather than a remote satellite.

Interview
Dominic Papa: Lessons in practice
Director at S333 Architecture + Urbanism

In the UK, modernist housing experiments of the 20th century are typically portrayed as profoundly flawed in terms of urbanism. What do you think are the key lessons that have been learned from those projects?

It's important to start by saying that there are a lot of positive qualities that we can still learn from in terms of architecture. A majority of modernist housing was organised around the repetition of standard morphological types. Therefore, we had buildings that did not respond to ground or orientation particularly well, and with the landscape being treated as purely the leftover space between the architecture. As a result, we have now ended up with a reactionary response as the pendulum swings too far the other way, whereby everything has to define a street, even where streets are not sustainable.

So often the problem is not in the building itself or that the buildings have been set back from the street, it's in the spaces between. When working with residents of high-rise buildings, you hear that once people get through their front doors they often love their flats, there's something nice about living high up, with large windows and long views, and they are often built to generous space standards. The challenge is getting from the street to their front door because there isn't a clearly defined sequence of spaces. This stems from the fact that landscape wasn't seen as being an important part of urbanism. We now understand how significant it is in providing orientation, legibility and defining how spaces are used, at certain times and by particular people.

You've worked outside the UK, in cities with detailed urban guidelines which define maximum building envelopes or specific ground-floor uses. Has this been helpful in delivering more successful architectural projects?

It's always helpful. Whilst the top-down approach is not always seen as politically acceptable in the UK, in the Netherlands, France and Germany where strong city governments are prevalent, they have used it to set clear, ambitious plans for the city. For example, at the beginning of the 20th century almost every Dutch town had a plan, even small towns of around a quarter of a million inhabitants. We have plenty of similarly sized towns in the UK that would benefit from a coordinated approach.

Ground-floor uses are also really important and, in order to avoid the same uses, proliferating cities benefit from a strategy at the wider scale that considers which amenities are needed. Many parameter plans used in large masterplans fail to accommodate flexibility, for example, to allow maisonettes or shops or workspace to be accommodated within a taller ground floor and to enable change over time. It's also important to consider how that is differentiated across a larger urban area to enable variance.

For many people, urban design has become restricted to the description of robust materials or a proximity to the street. Thinking at multiple scales is important and how a certain design is contributing to the larger neighbourhood in the amenities it offers, and also in how it is differentiated as a type. Differentiation is important, as it brings legibility, orientation and identity.

Many historical typologies are considered successful because they have proved to be adaptable over the centuries, but maybe we need different typological solutions in contemporary cities to deal with the conditions and increased densities?

The reason why some historic typologies have proven to be so adaptable is because they are spatially specific but functionally flexible; similarly sized rooms organised around clear circulation with structural flexibility. As the home has become increasingly cellular with a fixed idea of the family unit and how people should use them, it has become more and more inflexible. En suite bathrooms and small box rooms restrict the potential for the plan to adapt to the family needs and the family becomes atomised to the dark recesses of the plan.

Housing is highly regulated, probably more so than any other building genre, and that's constraining, and yet housing is also one of the most malleable genres. We require increasingly varied ways of living, whether it's lateral living, duplex or house, mansion block or courtyard, gallery or corridor access. How do we combine all of these into mixed-use buildings to form particular urban responses on increasingly constrained sites under developmental pressure?

Too often in proposals you see urban reasoning delivered through photos of the London vernacular streets and residential front doors, but, historically, streets didn't have to deal with the challenges of the contemporary city. There weren't cars parked on both sides of the road, they didn't have to accommodate multiple modes of traffic or deliveries. What we need to develop are the tools to set out how streets work and how they are differentiated across a larger grid and network at the city scale. We can't all have residential typologies delivering front doors to every street. We also have to design for mixed use and for those routes between the residential streets and the transport spines. Urbanists have those tools, but they're not part of the repertoire that architects or even cities are currently using.

When you start work on a project do you always question how it might support broader urban communities or neighbourhoods?

If it's a small site and the client has certain aspirations and a fixed financial model, then that brief is set. However, we always consider how the project is part of a dynamic process of urbanism. We look at pattern, grain, morphology and how that has evolved over time. We also consider what our project can contribute over time. Urbanism and typology allow you to be spatially specific whilst remaining flexible about functions.

In terms of estate regeneration, the challenge is often at an urban scale. It is a question of how to reintegrate estates into the surrounding neighbourhoods and wider city, how to open them up spatially and enable better connections with surrounding activities.

Housing is still seen as an issue of provision rather than city building; it is not seen as a critical element within urbanism that can create interesting and successful spaces in the city. Unlike shops, offices, schools and cultural buildings, which are genres that have been adapted to 21st-century

cities in sophisticated ways, housing is still somehow viewed separately.

In terms of density, the existing fabric of London isn't sufficiently dense to achieve the sustainable development that we now need. How can we plan for changes to density in cities?

In London, policy dictates that density is driven by accessibility, but with many developments the problem isn't accessibility, as there are other aspects constraining development. The nature of London's growth, with its very clear differentiation between central and suburban areas, means that new developments are often neighbouring London's historic two- to three-storey residential fabric. All of a sudden, anything over four storeys becomes a "tall building". This is exacerbated by the fact that much planning policy is based on a low-density understanding of housing. Using accessibility to promote density creates pressure points, and we lack the instruments in London to start to deliver a more consistent approach to scale. That's one of the reasons why you suddenly find 30-storey residential towers next to a train station. If we could understand a more consistent approach to density that builds on the identification of town centres, then that would start to address the problem, but for that we need a cross-borough, city-wide approach.

Reflecting on your European experience, is there more openness to experimentation at the urban scale within the European projects, and is that to do with the level of state intervention?

A strong state involvement in housing procurement helps the urban strategy, so it's interesting how the London boroughs are taking much more control now. They are developing affordable housing again and also looking at large areas of the city for coherent redevelopment projects, such as Tottenham High Road or the Olympic Legacy.

Architecture and urban design can't be separated from urbanism. In Europe you always have an architect on a large development team, whereas in the UK you attend briefings and there is the procurement team, project managers, the borough regeneration officer, you might have a design chief – but there's never an architect. If you go to Paris, Brussels or Hamburg, architects are very much part of development discussion at an urban scale and are therefore able to bridge the gap between scales.

How successful are the tools of the urbanist: parameter plans and design codes? Are they the right tools or have you used other approaches in different countries?

The issue with design codes and parameter plans all too often is that they are too static – do this and use that. Urbanism, by its very nature, is dynamic and responsive and therefore the issue is a question of value strategy and implementation. Parameter plans should establish the broad reasoning and argument for value propositions and how quality, character, consistency and hierarchy rather than rigid building heights and setbacks can deliver that. It should set the principles for diversification, integration and synergy, set against a background of changing conditions and emerging opportunities. If they are too dogmatic, then the richness and diversity one is striving for can quickly disappear. Urban design guidelines need to reflect this too and show the key design decisions necessary to successfully achieve the ambitions set by the principles. These also require a hierarchy: "must haves", "strongly encourage" and "good to have".

Design codes are too often enforcing almost a catalogue of urban elements rather than being developed as a tool to enable.

The downside with them is when codes and instruments lead to standardisation rather than effective design processes. For example, currently in London there is an overreliance on a simple perimeter block strategy that fails to address many of the most challenging developmental conditions. In the absence of the ideal conditions that support the perimeter block, little dynamic guidance for the design of family housing remains. This can also be seen with the emphasis on high streets where all the developmental and movement pressure gets focused onto one system. This constrains plots and restricts the spatial diversification that might be needed to sustain and integrate an area at a larger neighbourhood scale.

With perimeter blocks you end up putting too much pressure on a singular courtyard space, whilst a more open structure enables interesting opportunities to layer diverse elements so you might include a cinema or a school within the depth of a plot. In Hamburg you find very large urban blocks that actually reduces the number of streets. It utilises different strategies for privacy and clear access to residences. I visited one and at its centre it had an old pen factory and a community garden, as well as a number of play areas. It is a good illustration of how our current ideas about the relationship between urban form, mixed use and housing are too restrictive.

So one of the key issues around urbanism is the long timescales involved and the need for adaptability and flexibility in use. What tools can the urbanist develop that will adjust to changing economic conditions and social norms?

The art is how the plan can adapt. It should illustrate the ambition to enable stakeholders to engage proactively, particularly with its edges, but it must also be able to adapt to itself. So how do you set those principles? How do you set those overarching ambitions? This is where typology becomes interesting because typology doesn't define function or height, it talks about urban architecture and describes certain qualities and values about ambition and hierarchy and transparency, for example. This is somewhere between the strategic framework and architectural design and can give the robustness whilst maintaining flexibility for stakeholders and developers to understand where their opportunities are, but ensures that the local authority can retain control over the principles. ∎∎∎∎

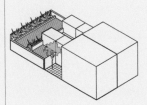 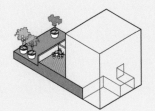 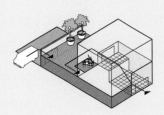 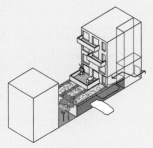

Buffer 1
Mixed uses set back from the residential accommodation give the opportunity for family houses at ground and first-floor level. Communal space is arranged at first-floor level behind the private terrace.

Buffer 2
Mixed uses on the ground floor. The deep floor plate and high ceiling heights allows for the private first-floor terrace to be separate from the communal courtyard.

Buffer 3
Mixed uses onto the street, with service access from the rear, enables communal or private roof terraces above.

Access and Parking
Car parking is decked over at the centre of the plot. A visually permeable, but secure ground floor, gives access to parking and communal terrace. Thresholds between private and communal are resolved with changes in level or clearly defined boundaries, balancing privacy and security.

5.0.6

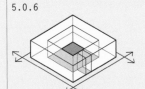 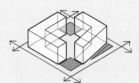 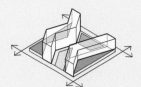 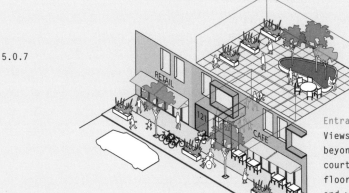

Communal space block scale
1: Clearly defined perimeter block, puts great pressure on central courtyard to differentiate spaces.

2: Looser block forms can integrate spaces inside and outside the perimeter, delivering a rich sequence of thresholds and communal spaces.

3: Form contributes to the differentiation of communal spaces and level changes help distinguish degrees of privacy.

4: Combinations of slab and tower create opportunities for gardens, courtyards and roof terraces, promoting balance between community life and needs of different users.

5.0.7

Entrance
Views through from the street to the communal courtyard beyond add to the quality of street and security of courtyards. Floor-to-ceiling height for ground floors enables flexibility among uses. Generous and welcoming apartment foyers create a sense of arrival and activity.

Dominic Papa is a director at S333 Architecture + Urbanism who, having established a reputation in the Netherlands and Europe with the practice's housing projects and being shortlisted for the Mies van der Rohe award, opened a London office in 2008. Dominic continues to advocate scaleless thinking, the potential in urban living and that architecture is urbanism through a wide range of projects, funded research, postgraduate teaching at the Architectural Association and as the chair of Islington design review.

5.1
Housing and crèche, Switzerland
Sergison Bates Architects + Jean-Paul Jaccaud Architectes

Country	Switzerland
Location	Geneva
Client	La Fondation de la Ville de Genève pour le logement social
Cost	€12.7m
Funding	Public
Units	17 apartments
Scale	8 storeys
Mixed uses	Crèche
Tenures	100% subsidised rent
Key dates	Competition 2006, completion 2011
Procurement	Traditional contract for the construction stages

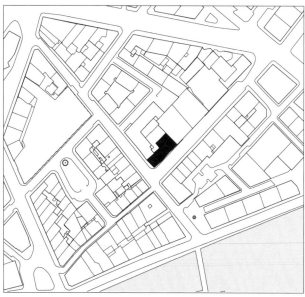

5.1.0 Location plan, scale 1:2000

At the heart of this project is a building that seeks to mediate between two distinct urban situations. On one side is the consistent urban texture of Geneva's Rue Rousseau, with buildings of significant presence such as the Ecole Ménagère des Jeunes Filles by Philippe Barras and Alexandre Camoletti, and on the other the Mont-Blanc/Cendrier centre, a 1950s tower and podium complex by Marc Saugey. The new building absorbs a number of spatial and volumetric elements, including the podium, arcade and faceted tower forms of Saugey's building, and continues the street edge and tripartite ordering of the Ecole Ménagère. Like a puzzle assembled from a number of building blocks carefully placed together, this new building has been developed from specifics of its place within Geneva, yet the urban moves it makes and problems it addresses are universal.

Commissioned by La Fondation de la Ville de Genève pour le logement social (the Geneva foundation for social housing), this project is formed of 18 social housing apartments and a crèche for 80 children. It was won through a competition held in 2006 by Sergison Bates Architects and Jean-Paul Jaccaud Architectes and completed in 2011.

As the new form seeks to stitch and weave itself into the texture of the city, the façade responds with a rich and layered assembly of finely stacked elements. The architects wanted to create a façade that presented its structure, giving a sense of permanence and weight to the wall. As a result, there is an expression of solidity that contributes to the definition of the urban blocks and a sense of enclosure and protection – the prerequisites for the creation of a feeling of home.

The vertical emphasis given to the façades echoes the typical frontages of the 18th- and 19th-century city and the podium height of the neighbouring Saugey towers. At a greater scale, the vertical ordering of top, middle and base, each responding to their corresponding use, increases daylight penetration and achieves continuity with adjacent building lines. The precast concrete elements have a polished finish, similar to a worn, creamy, grey stone. They are stacked in large "T" and "M" shapes to create a monolithic surface. Canvas blinds and light bronze anodized windows lend depth within the surface, revealing the activity

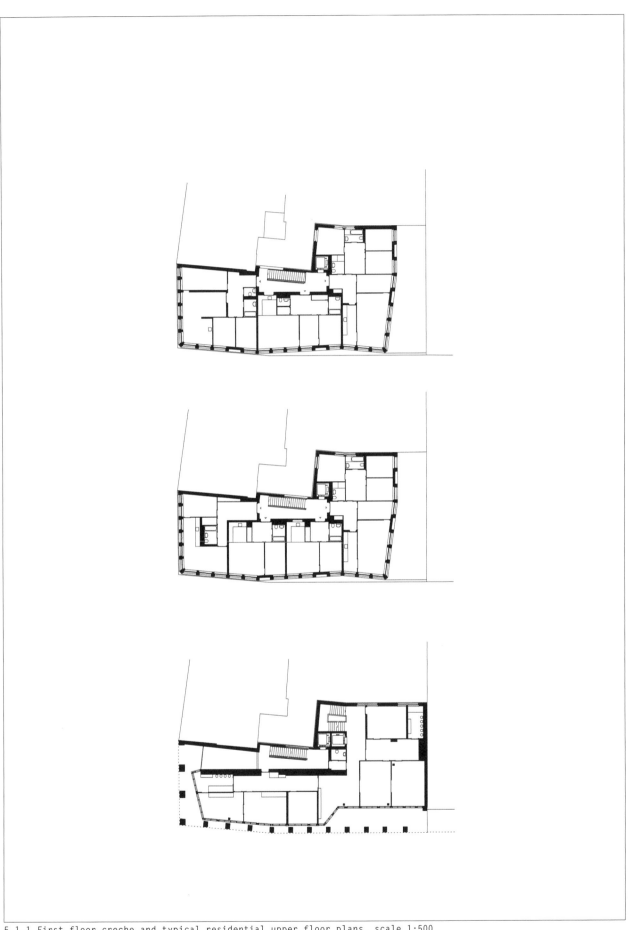

5.1.1 First floor creche and typical residential upper floor plans, scale 1:500

of occupation within the subtly shifting order of the tectonic façade.

Like the small courtyards coming throughout the St Gervais district of Geneva, noted for their atmosphere of intimacy and neighbourliness, access to the apartments is via an alley off the Rue Rousseau, leading to a small open court, with gallery access providing a shared semi-private threshold between apartments. Apartments are organised around the perimeter on all four sides, with central halls connecting the principal rooms in a continuous spatial sequence.

The building is inserted into the existing urban structure of arcades, covered walkways, alleys and yards, with a variety of openings and routes that create a sense of permeability within a dense city block. A new arcade extends the covered pavement established by Saugey's 1950s blocks, making it possible to walk down the length of Rue de Cendrier under cover. Just as the entrance to the Community Information Centre has the familiar detail of a shopfront, so too the entrance to the crèche is reminiscent of the open-air passages experienced as "cut-throughs" in Saugey's Mont-Blanc centre. A long view through the crèche foyer is created to the rear courtyard, which also provides a shaded and secure play space for the children.

In the same way that the activities of the crèche are brought into the view of the passerby at ground level, further openness is achieved at the second-floor level where a full length, open-sided veranda links each of the playrooms together to form a gallery of activity and energy.

Audible from the street below when opened and shaded, the veranda makes a highly visible addition to city life, contributing as it does to the essence of the city, a place to live and call home.

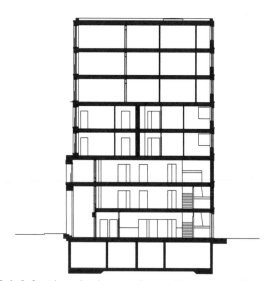

5.1.2 Section showing creche on first three floors with apartments above, scale 1:500

5.1.3 Façade design expressed mix of uses and responds to historic context

5.1.4 Family living space

5.1.5 Communal access route appropriated by residents

5.2
Kings Crescent, UK
Karakusevic Carson Architects + Henley Halebrown

Country	UK
Location	Hackney, London
Client	London Borough of Hackney
Cost	£60m phase one
Funding	Cross-subsidy funding
Units	765 dwellings: 490 new homes, refurbishment of 275 existing
Scale	5-12 storeys
Density	200 d/ha
Mixed uses	Café, retail and community centre
Tenures	50% affordable, 50% market sale
Key dates	Phase 1 planning November 2013, completion June 2017
Procurement	Design and build, tender at Stage 4 with full specification

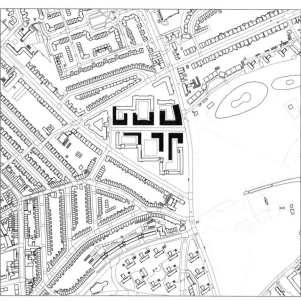

5.2.0 Location plan, scale 1:10000

This project involves the comprehensive redevelopment and refurbishment of Kings Crescent Estate in the London Borough of Hackney and is a significant part of the borough's wider estate regeneration programme. Karakusevic Carson Architects was appointed to lead a team of architects that included Henley Halebrown Rorrison and muf architecture/art to work on the public realm and landscape design. The first phase of the project includes 273 new homes and 101 refurbished homes.

The Kings Crescent Estate lies within an attractive part of west Hackney between Stoke Newington, Clissold Park and the broad, leafy streets of neighbouring Islington. On the estate, many properties had suffered from poor maintenance and public spaces lacked hierarchy and activity. As a result, the estate felt inward-looking and disconnected from the surrounding townscape. Previous attempts at redeveloping the estate had failed and, following partial demolition, no work had been undertaken for over 15 years. Working with Hackney Council, the design team developed a wider masterplan of 765 homes, which involved the refurbishment of 101 existing homes, the creation of 273 new homes in the first phase and the development of a generous landscape scheme. The second phase will deliver similar numbers.

Key to the project's development was the vital and intensive engagement with residents in order to identify their aspirations for a new neighbourhood and understand the issues that have affected the estate in recent years. This involved regular meetings between the council, its designers and the residents' steering group, as well as a number of public consultation events involving the wider estate and district. From the outset, the approach was to seek to reintegrate the estate with its surrounding townscape of Victorian streets and public spaces. Ultimately, it was proposed that this could be achieved by creating a series of robust partial courtyard blocks that combine existing and proposed buildings, as well as creating a series of well-defined and overlooked streets and public spaces connected through the site.

The original design for Kings Crescent Estate contributed significantly to its historical problems. Completed in 1971, it is typical of estates of this period,

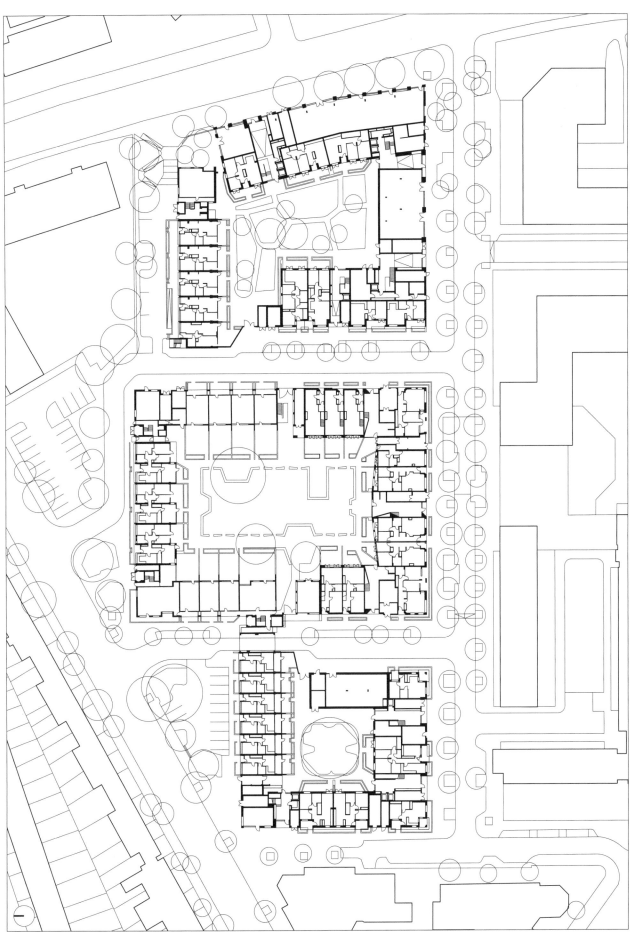

5.2.1 Ground-floor plan, scale 1:1000

ground-floor garages and long balconies with multiple entry points contributed to a maze-like atmosphere; it also gave the estate an introverted nature compared to the surrounding streets, which was compounded by the arrangement of the existing buildings. These issues were not reasons for demolition of existing blocks, but instead they were addressed through an intensive refurbishment strategy. Garages are being converted to homes, reconnecting the estate to its streets and addressing the poorly defined public spaces that had previously lacked passive surveillance. With the division of the long corridors, entry sequences are being provided that are more secure and create well-defined areas in which neighbours can socialise. In addition, the project includes extensive improvements to the public realm that opens up the estate to its neighbours and to the adjacent park. Generous balconies and winter gardens are being added to provide each existing home with its own outside space and improved thermal performance.

The design of the three new buildings responds to both the dominant massing of the existing estate, as well as the Victorian townscape of the surrounding terraced and semi-detached housing to the west, whilst maximising views of Clissold Park to the east. The buildings vary in scale from five to 12 storeys, while a number of key principles are repeated across plots, including front door-accessed ground-floor homes, generous communal entrances and the incorporation of large amenity spaces for family units. They include 79 homes at affordable rent, 36 shared ownership and 158 private sale homes; when combined with the refurbished homes, this results in half-social and half-private homes across the estate. A combination of high-quality materials with robust, considered detailing aims to ensure that the buildings sit comfortably in their varied context and allows them to age gracefully. The architectural approach aims to create successful higher density living whilst delivering a refinement of detail that lends elegance to the proportion of the façades and a clarity to the public realm.

The third fundamental part of the regeneration are the streets and open spaces, where Karakusevic Carson Architects worked with muf. A wide central avenue running east to west will provide a new artery connecting the

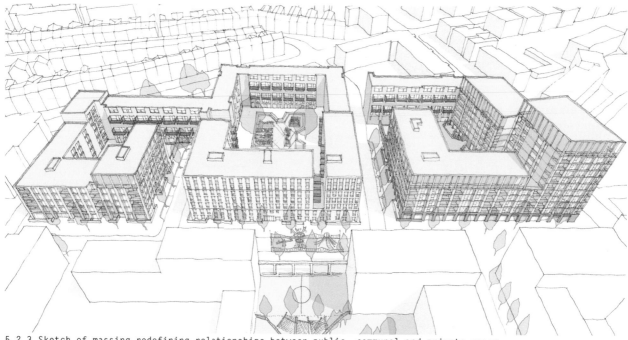

5.2.3 Sketch of massing redefining relationships between public, communal and private space

street grain of Islington with Clissold Park. An existing community garden is to be maintained and enhanced, and pockets of play throughout the scheme will encourage children and families to reclaim and enjoy the landscape. New public uses have been designed to cater for both the existing and emerging communities, and to improve the experience of the public realm.

Fundamental to the project is the council's commitment that the improvements are being made throughout the estate, and that quality of design and specification should be maintained whatever the nature of tenancy. The contractor developers involved in the project paid a lump sum to Hackney Council and then took over the leasehold of private flats, selling them at the market rate to fund the construction. Hackney Council has retained the freehold and will be managing the entire estate across all tenures.

Crucially, this project renovates and ameliorates the setting of the existing homes, the new buildings mirroring the scale of ambition of the original estate whilst successfully addressing the opportunities and failings of the surrounding urban fabric.

5.2.4

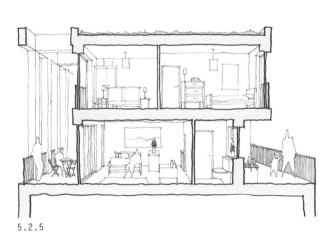

5.2.5

5.2.4 Render of view from Clissold Park of entrance to new street

5.2.5 Sketch through upper level social housing units with generous external space

5.2.6 Unit plan, scale 1:200

5.2.6

5.3
Paspoel Anders, Belgium
S333 Architecture + Urbanism

Country	Belgium
Location	Tongeren
Client	WoonZo
Cost	€23m
Funding	Flemish government
Units	192 apartments
Scale	3-8 storeys
Density	121 units/ha
Mixed uses	Community centre
Tenures	100% social rent
Key dates	Design 2012, construction 2016-21
Procurement	Housing association-led development

5.3.0 Location plan, scale 1:5000

S333 won this project in 2012 through the innovative Flemish State architect procurement process established to prioritise good design and to offer opportunities to emerging practices. The process required architects to submit their portfolios along with a short written response to a project brief and from this five offices were then paid to produce a sketch design.

The site lies on the outskirts of the historic city of Tongeren in a residential neighbourhood characterised by two-storey semi-detached houses with small front and back gardens. Three nine-storey blocks dominate the site and are surrounded by an undifferentiated landscape lacking in quality. High maintenance costs and poor living conditions, both due to substandard build quality, led the small housing association to look at demolition and redevelopment of the site. In order to enable all existing residents to remain living there throughout the process, the new urban arrangement had to be phased so that the construction of new homes was completed prior to the demolition of the three blocks. This was made more challenging by the Roman remains on the site, which meant that the new buildings were also confined to the exact outline of the existing blocks and basement car park.

S333 took this opportunity to reorganise the site, introducing a new civic space, communal gardens and a pedestrian street through the centre of the area, all animated by regular front doors. By clarifying access and movement, and by articulating meaningful transitional spaces between the public areas and private outdoor spaces, the project delivers a successful spatial strategy that integrates the project with its context and transforms the setting of the neighbouring terraced houses.

The architect's approach broadens the understanding of housing beyond being purely an issue of provision by also considering it as the basis for successful family environments. The project considers the relationship between building and resident at three equally important scales. The first is the quality of the floor plan for living, the second is the quality of collective space at the scale of the block and how it links to the street, and the third is the quality of neighbourhood life around a group of blocks that supports the inhabitants.

5.3.1 Cut-away axonometric showing site

In this project, much emphasis has been placed on making external space that feels secure and fosters the opportunity for inhabitants to meet and interact. Lobby areas are generous. External access galleries are not only considered as a corridor for access, but as generous transitional spaces that can be personalised and inhabited.

The natural tendency to move diagonally across the site from the north-east corner to the south-west corner is embedded in the sequence of interconnected spaces that frame everyday journeys from public to private and chance meetings between residents. Exterior spaces are provided for all age groups, ranging from secure play areas for children, recreational areas for teenagers, allotment gardens for families and communal courtyard spaces for the elderly.

The "grid-like" organisation extends to the edges of the site, creating a strong but complementary contrast to the spatial logic of the surrounding suburban context. Existing trees were kept and provide protection from the wind for a children's play area. New trees reinforce lines of movement, act as semipermeable shelterbelts and characterise the three communal areas in the plan.

Within the low-rise linear blocks and medium-rise point blocks, a variety of residential units are provided. The layout of the units is simple and straightforward, following strict guidelines overseen by the Belgium ministry of social housing. The opportunity to bring design innovation to the layout of internal rooms and circulation spaces is limited. However, each unit is provided with a private outdoor space, internal corridors are minimised and wherever possible living spaces are optimised by combining storage with circulation spaces.

At ground level, house types vary depending on the conditions between public and private spaces, relationship to pedestrian streets, play areas, civic spaces and courtyards. S333 applied similar considerations to the design of the access galleries, which on the northern and eastern side of the linear blocks expand at moments to create areas to sit in the sunshine, while they pull away on the southern side of façades to offer privacy to south-facing units.

The project demonstrates how a loose arrangement of "block form" can offer a viable alternative to the hermetic perimeter block, integrating typological diversity and a rich sequence of thresholds and communal spaces. As with many of the other regeneration projects in this book, the architects had to develop a complex choreography of phased rehousing, demolition and construction, in this case in order to ensure that all the residents can continue to live on the site throughout the five-year redevelopment period.

5.3.2 Tongeren Paspoel plaza view

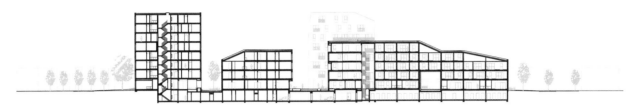

5.3.3 Section, scale 1:1000

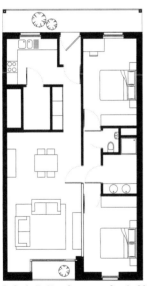

5.3.4 Unit plan, scale 1:200

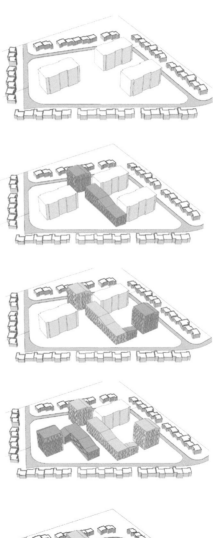

5.3.5 Phasing diagram

5.4
Darbishire Place, UK
Níall McLaughlin Architects

Country	UK
Location	Tower Hamlets, London
Client	Peabody trust
Cost	£2.3m
Funding	Housing association
Units	13
Scale	3-4 storeys
Mixed uses	None
Tenures	100% affordable
Key dates	2007-2014
Procurement	Design and build

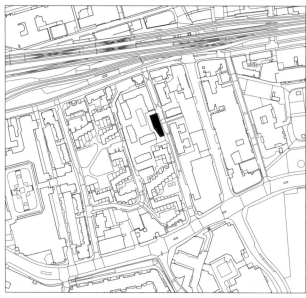

5.4.0 Location plan, scale 1:5000

Darbishire Place, at Peabody's Whitechapel Estate in East London, completes an ensemble of six housing blocks surrounding an internal courtyard – the original block having been destroyed during the second world war. The commission was the result of a study that was carried out by Níall McLaughlin Architects and Haworth Tompkins into the feasibility of developing 42 sites owned by Peabody that were previously considered too small for viable development. With a budget in keeping with typical Peabody affordable housing projects, the scheme is comprised of 13 new one- to four-bedroom homes. The design respects the massing and characteristics of the existing buildings on the estate and continues the idea of open corners, promoting easy pedestrian access and views between the courtyard and the surrounding streets.

Urban design was carefully considered, with the eastern façade of the new block aligning with the existing buildings onto John Fisher Street and with Block E to the north, while the south end relates closely to the adjacent Block J. The new building has a chamfered south-west corner, allowing views and light into the courtyard and creating a new pedestrian link between the spaces.

Planning constraints were within normal planning policy. The estate is not located in a conservation area; however, the conservation officer took a particular interest due to the significance of the surrounding Peabody housing blocks, which were designed by Henry Darbishire in the 1870s. The existing blocks are of five storeys with repetitive window patterns reflecting their internal layouts. The openings are formed with brick reveals that are painted white, adding to the buildings' particular Italianate character.

The façades in the new building make a respectful reference to the surrounding buildings with the contrast between the external brick skin and the deep window reveals repeated and accentuated. The reveals are formed from prefabricated Glass Reinforced Concrete (GRC) blocks and occur around each window and balcony. These deep reveals taper to a fine edge, creating sharp repetitive frames and a compelling play of light and shadow across the façades.

The main entrance is from the courtyard side of the building, in keeping with the other blocks. It leads into a lobby that opens up towards the lift and the bottom of

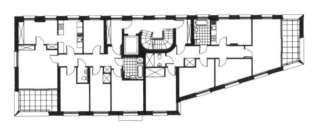

5.4.1 Floor plans, scale 1:500

5.4.2

5.4.3

the staircase. The central circulation space, which tenants pass through every day, is flooded with natural light from the windows above. The staircase winds its way up around a dramatic central void, which creates visual connections between the landings.

The internal layouts are arranged around the single stair and lift core that provides access to 13 units over five floors. Most of their habitable rooms are oriented south or west, away from John Fisher Street where windows are subject to traffic noise. The building has a wheelchair-accessible flat to the north of the ground floor.

The large balconies to the new flats are internal to maintain the solid and object-like character of the new building. They are open to at least two sides with nearly full-width openings and a low solid balustrade to maximise daylight into the living rooms located adjacent to them.

Located on a narrow and constrained site with a strong architectural identity, the project successfully delivers family-sized homes of architectural generosity, the larger homes having triple-aspect living rooms. The conversation between the new and historic materials also delivers a scheme of high-quality materiality and architectural detailing.

5.4.4

5.5
Bacton Estate, UK
Karakusevic Carson Architects

Country	UK
Location	Gospel Oak, London
Client	London Borough of Camden
Cost	Phase 1 £18m, Phase 2 projected £80m
Funding	Local authority, cross-subsidy funding
Units	314
Scale	2-8 storeys
Density	166 d/ha
Mixed use	Commercial units 259 sq m
Tenures	50% affordable, 50% Private sale target, reviewable financial model at each phase
Key dates	2011, Phase 1 completion 2016
Procurement	Two-stage tender, design and build with open book

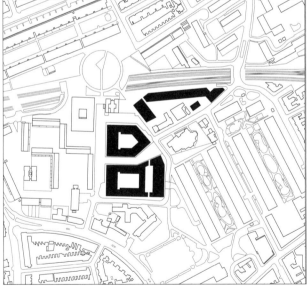

5.5.0 Location plan, scale 1:5000

In mid-2011, Karakusevic Carson Architects found themselves in the unusual position of being approached directly by the residents of the Bacton Estate in Gospel Oak, Camden. The residents had been campaigning for the regeneration of their estate for the past 10 years and were spearheading a competition with the council and their project managers. The residents were pivotal in the interview and selection process, assuming a leadership role in the development that would continue throughout the project.

The existing low-rise estate, built in the 1960s and covering 1.4 ha, had significant problems including poor maintenance, leaking flat roofs and damage to existing timber cladding. Working in tandem with the residents and Camden Council, Karakusevic Carson Architects sought to rectify the mistakes of the past and reconnect the neighbourhood with the surrounding area in a scheme that would see the creation of 314 mixed-tenure homes, with a focus towards family homes that would maintain and strengthen the community.

Bacton is a success story of Camden's community investment programme, a 15-year plan to invest in schools, homes and community facilities. The borough is seeking to raise around £300m through innovative use of its land in order to develop, maintain and refurbish its housing stock as a direct consequence of a capital funding gap following reduced government funding. The plan aims to deliver over 3,000 homes, of which half will be classed as genuinely affordable.

Following careful planning, the regeneration of the estate is expected to be cost neutral, with medium-density private-sale housing directly cross-subsidising the socially rented and shared ownership housing. The process will be split across two phases, organised in such a way to ensure the vast majority of residents will not have to move more than once. The phasing programme will also ensure a mix of tenures and unit types within each stage, addressing both overcrowding and underoccupancy across the estate in order to find a balance for existing residents.

Going beyond the bare minimum of consultation the Bacton Estate represents a closely monitored relationship with the residents. Karakusevic Carson

5.5.1 Ground-floor plan, scale 1:1000

5.5.2 Existing estate

Architects presented residents and Camden Council with a set of materials early on in the process, along with trips to brickmaking factories in order to assist with the visualisation of the project. No fewer than seven consultation meetings took place prior to planning submission, which were well attended by existing residents, freeholders and the local community. Regular meetings with the tenants' and residents' association and Camden's maintenance team carried on beyond planning stage, with particular attention paid to high-quality and robust materials with longevity in mind.

The residents generally requested low-rise housing and homes with new streets to replace unpopular access desks. However, the regeneration team and local community proved open to initial proposals for a network of interconnected streets with three- to five-storey family housing. By utilising the street edges and maximising the site opportunities, the team found a varied approach to density was the most suitable. This culminated in a large range of home types and sizes, ranging from one-bedroom apartments through to four- and five-bedroom homes and family maisonettes.

5.5.3 New homes address previously ill-defined street

The design of the landscape and public realm also represents the result of a complex process to distinguish between private, semi-private and public space. Communal and private entrances at street level with double-height lobbies encourage activity within the public realm, while rooftop private amenity space, recessed and external balconies ensure open spaces across the development. The perimeter blocks look down on landscaped gardens and play spaces, which are shared by all residents.

Site issues were also a major design consideration to contend with, including acoustic issues along the northern edge where the high-speed rail link runs between Euston and the north-west. The site is also adjacent to two listed buildings: the Grade I-listed St Martin's Church and the Grade II-listed French School. The aim is to bring the church back into the heart of the new network of streets as a clear visual element to the community. The visibility of the church is enhanced by a careful approach to massing, with nearby buildings sloping down to promote its townscape significance. A new, pedestrianised street opens up views to the church and establishes a new public space for the local residents and wider community.

Responding to a demand for family homes, the scheme is an expression of contemporary family life including front gardens, communal squares and generous window openings. Despite this requirement, the project is designed as tenure blind across the site and across the phasing programme. Since the golden era of Camden's very own modernist architects' department under Sydney Cook, the Bacton estate represents the first social housing Camden has commissioned in nearly 30 years.

  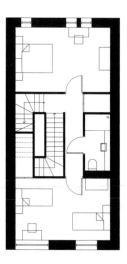 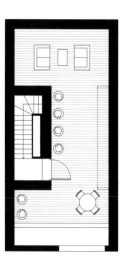

5.5.4 Unit plan, scale 1:200

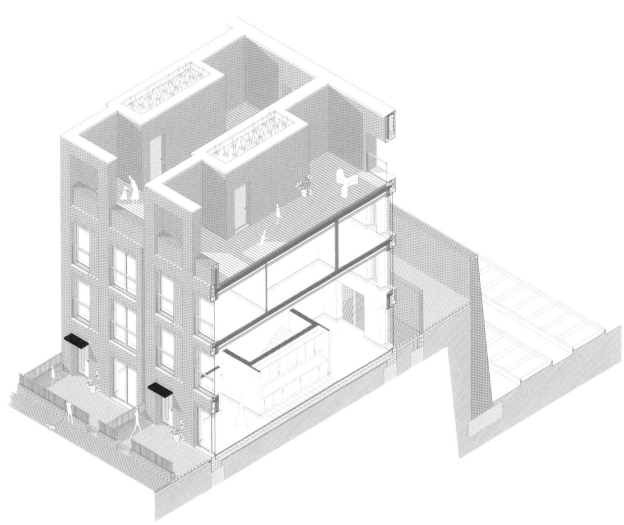

5.5.5 Axonometric through townhouse showing relationship to railway

5.5.6 Townhouses animate street with regular front doors

5.6
Almshouse, UK
Witherford Watson Mann Architects

Country	UK
Location	Bermondsey, London
Client	United St Saviour's charity
Cost	Undisclosed
Funding	Undisclosed
Units	57
Scale	5 storeys
Density	200 d/ha
Tenures	100% social rent
Key dates	Planning January 2016, completion expected 2019
Procurement	Under discussion

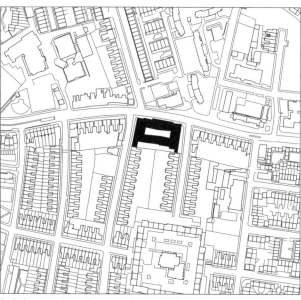

5.6.0 Location plan, scale 1:5000

In recent years the accommodation of elderly residents within urban environments has become a focus for research within planning and design. As people live longer, affordable housing for the elderly is being pushed further from city centres, due to pressures of population and land value. Isolation and loneliness have become significant problems, and innovative responses are required in order to build at greater density, but at the same time provide the areas in which residents can share and socialise. Great care is required both in the management of the relationships between privacy and engagement with surroundings, and between individual residents' homes and communal space.

Designed by Witherford Watson Mann Architects, the development will provide the long-established United St Saviour's charity with its third almshouse. The first was established in Southwark in 1584 (subsequently relocated to Purley) and the second built in Bankside in 1752. The scheme realises affordable housing that will be available for Southwark residents who are over the age of 70. As an extra-care development, it will provide independent living accommodation for around 90 older people, along with significant ancillary communal and public areas. The residential accommodation comprises 51 one-bedroom apartments and six two-bedroom apartments, varying between 50 and 82 sq m, depending on individual need. In addition to a community lounge and café, ground-floor communal facilities include a private residents' lounge, a cookery teaching space and a multi-use craft room. A laundry room, a bathing/therapy room, a hairdressing salon and meeting spaces will be situated on the first floor.

The almshouse will be located on the site of a vacant, post-war nursing home and the local high street, with various small shops and amenities, in the direct vicinity. Situated between the fine-grained Thorburn Square conservation area of predominantly two- and three-storey houses and the larger, varying scale of villas and post-war housing blocks, the almshouse needs to respond to two distinct scales. The building rises to five storeys and is concave in form along Southwark Park Road, addressing the street and creating an inviting entrance. Generous communal areas – including the community lounge – are

5.6.1 Ground-floor plan, scale 1:500

5.6.2 Almshouse exterior

5.6.3 Almshouse courtyard

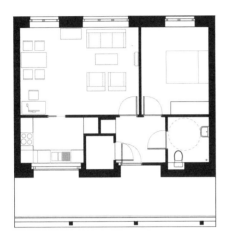

5.6.4 Unit plan, scale 1:200

arranged along this main elevation in two-storey glazed bays. These will be highly visible from the street and will be available for use by community groups. The building is organised around a central garden court, a response to the specialised requirements of the almshouse that will require a balance between active, sociable, shared spaces and individual privacy. It is the unifying focus of the building, with all residents approaching their apartments along a glazed walkway that opens onto the central residents' garden. The dual aspect community lounge and a café are entirely open to this garden space.

The garden court is bounded by a two-storey rear wing where the building steps down to meet the scale of the terraced housing on the side streets. Roof gardens on these lower volumes provide raised planting beds and outdoor rooms. The durable, highly crafted elevations are detailed to reflect the characteristics of the surrounding Victorian terraces. They form a strong presence on the street with a combination of textured, purple-brown brick, precast concrete lintels and cills, and timber-framed windows. Terracotta tiling is used to clad the set-back fifth storey and the gables to the side streets.

The design reinvents the almshouse typology to create a distinctively urban development that maximises its position on the local high street. The building is urban in nature and is active, open and in direct contact with the street. Loneliness has a huge impact on older people and the design creates opportunities for sharing and sociability throughout the almshouse.

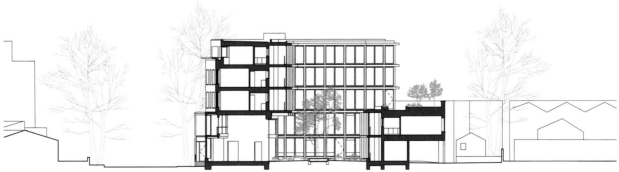

5.6.5 Section, scale 1:500

5.7
Tower Court, UK
Adam Khan Architects + muf architecture/art

Country	UK
Location	Hackney, London
Client	London Borough of Hackney
Cost	£37m
Funding	Local authority, cross-subsidy funding
Units	132
Scale	6-12 storeys
Density	188 d/ha
Tenures	78 private sale, 19 shared ownership and 33 social rented
Key dates	Design work completion July 2016, project completion anticipated 2019
Procurement	Design and build with construction tender at RIBA Stage 4A

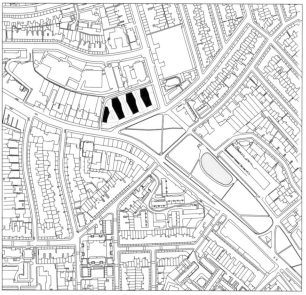

5.7.0 Location plan, scale 1:5000

Tower Court is at the head of Clapton Common in a busy and culturally diverse residential neighbourhood known for being home to Europe's largest Jewish Haredi community. The site is currently empty, following the demolition of a 1950s estate. The brief asks for high-density family living, accommodating both returning residents and large families. The scheme is self-financing, with private units cross-subsidising intermediate and social rent tenures. Hackney Council is the landowner and will retain the site in perpetuity.

Whilst the site was previously considered extremely constrained and in an area with some community tensions, the design team used these constraints and issues as opportunities to develop a proposal highly specific to place, comfortable for high-density family living and addressing the changing and culturally diverse needs in family housing. A very active process of engagement gathered vital intelligence from the outset, allowing a sustained set of conversations between and amongst the local communities, which was continued throughout the design process. A dialogue and design process brought together local communities who tend to be isolated from each other. This will manifest in the built scheme, where each courtyard is a healthy mix of tenure type and unit size.

In a complete integration of architecture and landscape, the public realm extends into the entrance lobbies, and the angled geometry of the blocks improves internal qualities of daylight, views and double aspect, but also shapes the courtyards as comfortable softly folding outdoor rooms. The mature trees are retained and have informed the positions of the building, forming a rich fourth elevation. The constraint of root protection zones are used to establish a deep-planted border to the housing, making a dignified, convincing clarification of public and private spaces which remain open and welcoming. The landscape is intensively shaped as a place of play opportunity and social encounter, a series of nine bespoke play bridges spanning the swales of the sustainable drainage.

The intensive consultation and design process with members of all local communities yielded significant results that are applicable to the Haredi community, large families from other communities, sharing groups and family life

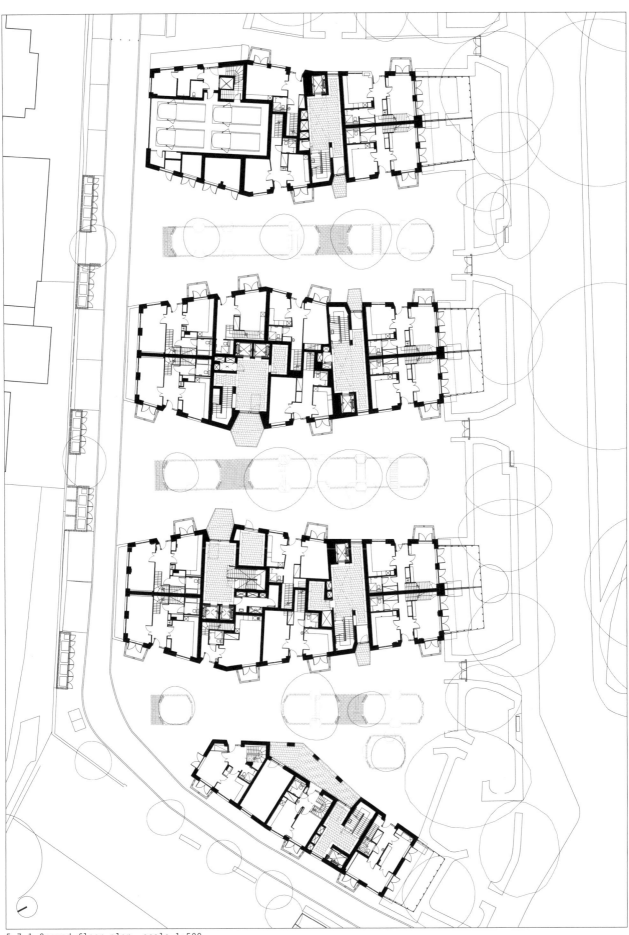

5.7.1 Ground-floor plan, scale 1:500

more generally. This common ground translated into a set of principles for designing generous and flexible family living. The flat layouts offer alternative ways of organising the use of rooms within the home, for example, by allowing two bedrooms to be connected to provide an additional large sociable space for festive occasions or play, or by making a wider internal staircase that can be lined to form a library or extra storage.

When living at density, it is critical that accommodation is of a high standard. Here, 78% of homes are dual-aspect. This has been achieved by building volumes that maximise the number of corner units, and for the maisonettes in the centre of the plan, a dual aspect scissor typology has also been developed. All family units in social rented and private tenures exceed the minimum space standards for dwellings sizes set out in the London housing supplementary planning guidance by a minimum of 10%, a generosity achieved through the careful design of a cost-efficient building form and footprint, with compact communal circulation spaces. The cores typically serve no more than four units per floor, and all cores are day-lit using borrowed light from the stair core. The compact layout allows a clear and direct relationship between the entrances and private front doors, as well as a sense of ownership with the shared entrance hall. This also delivers a highly efficient net-to-gross ratio.

By rejecting generic housing solutions and instead designing a project that responds to the specifics of place and people, a new piece of city can be made. This open-block typology has been developed to create homes that are dignified, comfortable, adaptable and socially sustainable.

5.7.2 Tower Court carved and sculpted courtyards

5.7.3 Tower Court scissor maisonette

5.7.4 Tower Court family maisonette

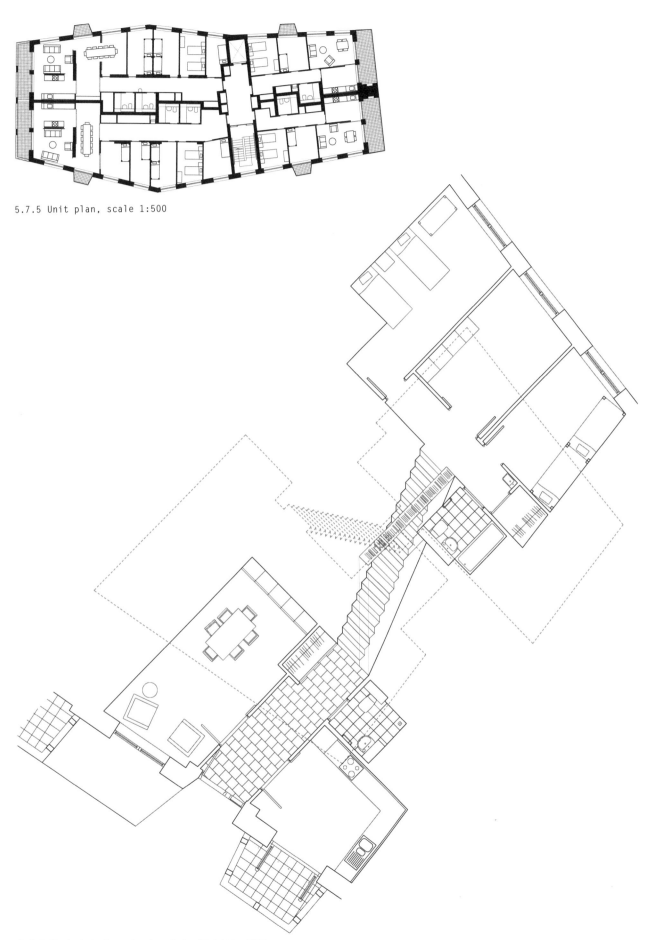

5.7.5 Unit plan, scale 1:500

5.7.6 Exploded plan showing interlocking units

5.8
Nightingale Estate, UK
Karakusevic Carson Architects + Stephen Taylor Architects + Henley Halebrown Rorrison + Townshend Landscape Architects

Country	UK
Location	Hackney, London
Client	London Borough of Hackney
Cost	£137m
Funding	Funded by land disposal and development partner agreement
Units	400
Scale	5-6 storeys and incorporation of existing 22-storey tower
Density	181 units per hectare
Mixed uses	232 sq m commercial, 62 sq m office space, 453 sq m community centre, 3 parks improved, 9 hectares of public realm improvements
Tenures	52 social rent, 72 shared ownership, 276 private sale (part of a borough-wide cross-funding strategy to build new affordable homes)
Key dates	Design 2015, planning 2017, construction 2018-22
Procurement	Design and build with architect to be novated. Design drawings taken to RIBA Stage 4A

5.8.0 Location plan, scale 1:5000

Karakusevic Carson Architects, in collaboration with Stephen Taylor Architects, Henley Halebrown Rorrison and Townshend Landscape Architects were appointed by the London Borough of Hackney for the final phase of regeneration of the Nightingale Estate. The community-led design process includes the delivery of 400 mixed-tenure homes, a new community facility, retail units and new public realm for the entire estate.

The estate is located north of Hackney Downs and has been undergoing regeneration since the early 1990s when six 22-storey towers previously dominated the townscape. Five towers were demolished in the early 2000s and one, Seaton Point, was refurbished and retained. Southern Housing Group developed the early phases of the regeneration process, resulting in low-rise low-density developments with streets dominated by car parking. The result is an estate formed of disparate streetscapes and building styles, from the tower to 1970s slab blocks and pitched-roofed 1990s suburban housing.

The aim of this masterplan is to provide a development that enhances connections between the existing disparate neighbourhoods within the estate through the introduction of a new north/south street grain linking the existing residential streets, the new development and Hackney Downs park to the south. An integrated approach to the design of the public realm and housing is centred on the creation of neighbourhood streets with residential entrance courts accessing a limited number of dual-aspect homes, providing a sociable, safe, entry sequence from street to home.

The design of the new streets contributes positively to the surrounding townscape, offering improved connectivity and street façades that complement the London vernacular. Generous Juliet windows, recessed balconies and a regular rhythm of bay windows highlight living rooms and kitchens, and express the human scale of the development within the composition of the street.

A common palette of materials is proposed across all of the new streets; handmade brickwork and precast concrete detailing provide quality and longevity. Architectural features and ground-floor communal entrances are highlighted through bespoke precast concrete

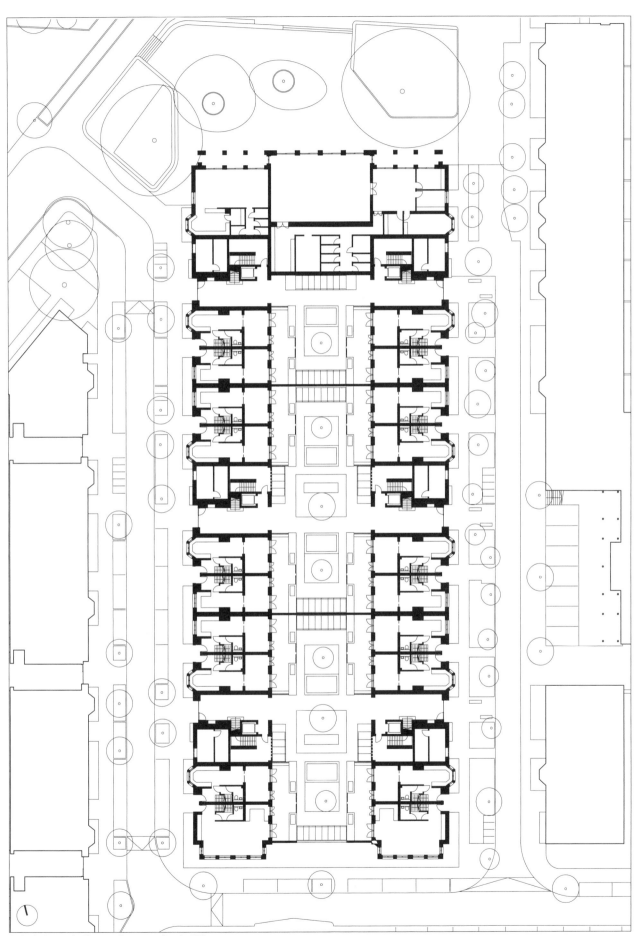

5.8.1 Ground-floor plan, scale 1:500

Urban responses and
challenging sites

5.8   Nightingale Estate, UK
Karakusevic Carson Architects + Stephen Taylor Architects +
Henley Halebrown Rorrison + Townshend Landscape Architects

147

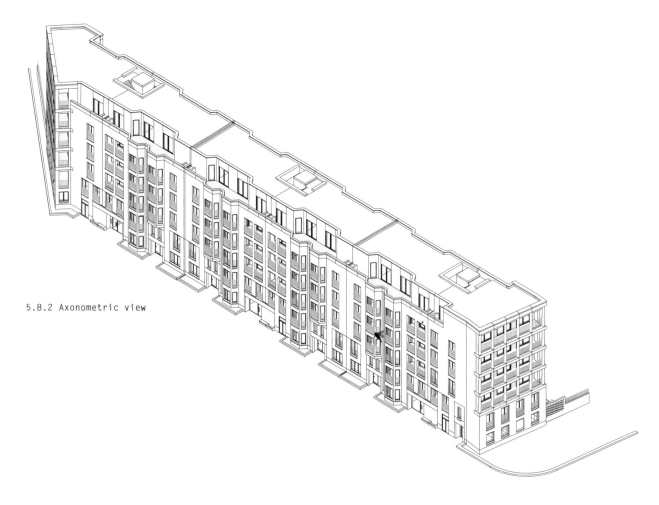

5.8.2 Axonometric view

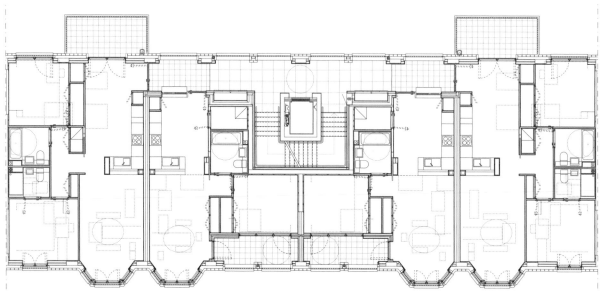

5.8.3 Unit plan, scale 1:200

cladding, which also forms benches and kerbs linking the buildings and their public realm.

The project is the result of an intensive residents' participation process, with weekly meetings held with the steering group during the design phase. Along with the residents, Hackney Council has shown a strong commitment to the long-term success of the Nightingale community and the delivery of an exemplar regeneration project that has the potential to form a new model for medium-rise, high-density housing and places the creation of a sociable residential street at its heart.

A return to an historic typology and a rigorously simple approach will provide a consistency currently lacking in the surrounding fabric; the familiarity of the streets and architecture re-establishing a familiar London environment.

5.8.4 Strong frontage introduced onto Hackney Downs Park

5.8.5 Reintroduction of neighbourhood streets

5.8.6 Communal entrance courtyards

Urban responses and
challenging sites

5.8   Nightingale Estate, UK
Karakusevic Carson Architects + Stephen Taylor Architects +
Henley Halebrown Rorrison + Townshend Landscape Architects

149

Interview
Rachel Bagenal
London Borough of Hackney

How are briefs formulated by Hackney for new housing projects?

The briefs are written by the regeneration team. We put a huge amount of work into getting them right. As the design manager, I work very carefully on this with the project managers and we spend a lot longer than a typical client at the early stages of the projects. Detailed work goes into understanding the site, the communities living there, those living around it and what we want out of a project.

There are so many pressures to consider: developing appropriate tenure mix in relation to housing need, complex viability testing and the pressure to deliver numbers of units. How is this dealt with in terms of delivering density or mixes of uses?

Our programme prioritises housing. Like elsewhere, Hackney has a crisis of housing supply and affordability. We need to use the land we own to build as much housing as we possibly can. We aren't frightened of density, but we do have to find what's right for each site to ensure that we are building great places to live. We work carefully with our architects on developing housing typologies that are appropriate for each context. We want our schemes to demonstrate that desirable features found in popular housing typologies, such as terraced houses, can be achieved in densely flatted developments.

How does Hackney manage its housing projects and all the team members?

Hackney writes the briefs, appoints the architects and employs them directly to design the schemes to a good level of detail. Only then is the project tendered to contractors developers.

Delivering well-designed and built housing schemes requires thought and hard work at all stages of the development process. We have put a lot of time into improving the way we manage projects at each stage – especially during construction.

Hackney appoints an employer's agent (including a quantity surveyor and clerk of works) at the start of the design process. They are there to ensure that what is designed gets built, participating in all stages of the process to ensure that they are buildable within budget. The employer's agent then works with us and the architects to produce a robust set of employer's requirements that specifies many details beyond planning. This involved approach means that the employer's agent and clerk of works understand the council's vision for the project and are well placed to protect the design after the scheme is tendered.

We encourage the contractor to take on our architects for the working drawings, as they are best placed to translate the design intent into the realised building and landscape. We are also exploring other ways to protect the design on a design and build contract – one idea is to retain a member of the original design team client-side. They would assist the Hackney project manager in reviewing contractor's proposals as they emerge, ensuring the integrity of the design isn't undermined.

Once the housing is built, it will be handed back to the council for management and maintenance into the future. This stage has its own challenges – if you build a beautiful building but nobody knows how to manage it, and if tenants don't know how to operate the equipment in their flats, then the reputation of the building can be hugely damaged.

How does Hackney select its architects?

We select our architects in a variety of ways. We have been using the GLA's architecture, design and urbanism panel for some schemes, OJEU for others and smaller design competitions for lower-value contracts.

The procurement process for architects has been refined over several years. Too many of these prioritise financial considerations over the qualitative aspects of bids. We have worked hard to ensure that we have a sophisticated and informed approach to choosing architects and that design skill is a priority. We always prioritise design over fee, using a 70% quality/30% price ratio when scoring

bids. The scope has been clarified to ensure that all bidders have a common understanding of what we are asking for. Bids are carefully evaluated by a panel that always includes design experts.

On many of our projects, we run a two-stage competition, where practices are invited to submit their initial response to the brief. Practices are then shortlisted solely on the basis of their design approach and invited to the next stage. It is only at this stage that the fee is factored into the evaluation.

We have found collaborations between more experienced practices with younger offices to be very successful, and we are now looking at running some smaller competitions to get some new talent involved. This will allow younger practices to have a chance and Hackney will benefit from architects building their first big project and the commitment you get from this.

It is important that architects challenge us as a client, just as we challenge them. We need them to question and test the brief. Dialogue, opinion and debate brings a richness to the process and I believe it ultimately results in a better design.

For me, it is hugely exciting to be working for a council that is building. As a client we are able to bring in other objectives that might be overlooked working in the private sector. We are working on land that is publically owned and we are building a legacy. Hackney usually retains the freehold and manages the projects across all the tenures, so we are investing in estates in the long term and making sure the building envelope is carefully detailed and built from high-quality robust materials that will ensure they can stand the test of time.

There are many projects from the 1960s and 1970s with failings from which we need to learn lessons. Would you agree that one of those lessons is about urbanism and the relationship between housing and the ground level or surrounding streetscape?

Whilst all our existing sites and estates are different, there are some recurring themes. The buildings themselves are often well designed, with good materials and generous space standards. The homes are frequently popular with residents but it is the urban plan that doesn't work – the way the buildings relate to the local neighbourhood and how the public realm and landscape have been maintained. This isn't helped by street clutter, excessive signage and ad-hoc parking arrangements that develop in poorly designed outdoor space. When estates do not look cared for, it has a massive impact on peoples' perceptions about where they live.

We feel that quality outdoor space is fundamental to the architecture and are working hard to encourage collaboration between the architect and landscape designers. On Tower Court, the buildings and spaces around them are being designed simultaneously; there is no line between inside and outside. We are learning from the mistakes of the past where we might have focused too much on the architecture and not thought carefully enough about the ground floor and landscape.

Repurposing garages is another way we can transform the ground floor on existing estates. On our Kings Crescent project we are converting garages into homes. Just the act of doing so will transform the buildings' relationship with the street and the experience at ground floor.

Do you think the role of the London Housing Design Guide can be prohibitive in terms of encouraging mix and innovation?

I am a supporter of the standards because they set a minimum. However, if everything is built to conform to them we will end up with a lot of identikit homes. The housebuilders like the standards because they provide a set of rules, they are quite conventional and they represent a saleable way of living. But if you want to do something extraordinary you can't just stick to the rules.

What is interesting about the Tower Court project is that Adam Khan Architects has been innovative in interpreting those standards, working on genuinely adaptable layouts that allow people to alter the way they inhabit their homes over time. The economics and social habits of living in London today means that the nature of the home is already changing. Who knows how we will live in 20 years' time?

The really exciting thing is that the public sector can build private housing that people want to buy. We are not just good at building council housing. We'd like to think that we're building housing that will be more desirable than what the standard housebuilders are offering. ▬▬▬

Rachel Bagenal's current role as a project manager delivering two high-profile regeneration schemes at Hackney Council follows a 10-year design career in central and local government. Rachel's four years as a design manager in the estate regeneration team at Hackney Council came after advising local authorities on how to create better buildings and spaces at Cabe.

Conclusion

Abigail Batchelor: Thinking differently
Associate, Karakusevic Carson Architects

The title of this book is deliberately provocative. For far too long, housing has been restricted by a limited range of procurement routes, housing tenures and typologies. From the persistence of old housing models to the unfulfilled reliance on the market, this book is a challenge to housing professionals, a new generation of students interested in public sector projects and those architects and urban designers interested in entering the sector to rethink current norms. It is also a challenge to the status quo. Housing is social and it must be a project in which we all share and stand up for; it is a human right rather than a typical commodity.

Our cities are places that can embrace, accommodate and sustain change. Previous generations of designers transformed our cities in response to major crises and fast-paced transformation. The only time that we have come close to building the numbers of homes needed in the UK was when national government was driving the process in the years after the second world war. That local authorities are again starting to control and willing to invest in the delivery of public housing is a positive sign. Whilst the economic conditions vary widely across London boroughs – not to mention the rest of the country – the fact that the state still owns large areas of land and has the possibility to invest in housing is a good start. However, in order to address the shortage of housing, it will need the borrowing powers to be able to respond adequately.

The state has a mixed track record in delivering housing, but there is no excuse for repeating the mistakes of the past, such as poor quality construction, a lack of resident involvement, the prioritising of quantity over quality and domineering architectural style and scale. Local authorities are in a unique position to manage the planning process and to deliver sites for housing construction. The case studies in this book demonstrate that they are also proving themselves to be innovative clients, developing robust procurement processes and delivering ambitious architecture and urbanism. They are starting to achieve more diversity and higher-quality homes than the market. Challenges of the electoral cycle and ideology will remain, but cross-party consensus could allow for longer-term planning, continuity of vision and insurance against the effects of economic downturns or uncertainty.

This book celebrates the role of the architect in enabling incremental change to existing homes and neighbourhoods. Summoning up the utopian spirit of previous generations, the case studies show architects across Europe are successfully addressing the failings of built fabric and realising the latent potential of housing estates and the communities who live there.

This publication shows that when architects work for, or closely with, the state, they can be a positive force in understanding existing housing, responding to residents' priorities, resolving challenging sites, creating innovative urban responses and achieving viable redevelopments. Learning from Europe and looking back at our own history, the case studies discussed in chapter three recognise that new forms of tenure, such as co-operatives, community land trusts and co-housing, offer alternative models that operate by varying degrees outside the market. Whilst not strictly social or public housing in the traditional sense of that word, and something of a niche market, they offer opportunities for the creation of homes through active participation by residents and investment in the life of their cities.

Architects are often criticised for prioritising personal stylistic preferences or for lacking sincerity in their relationships with local residents. However, the case studies in this book demonstrate how close collaboration with client groups and communities can deliver architectural generosity and regeneration with real benefits, whilst minimising the displacement, upheaval and disruption for existing communities. Good processes and committment are crucial to successful housing outcomes.

There is not only a shortage of homes in our cities but employment spaces are becoming increasingly scarce. Whilst the examples in this book are yet to rise to the challenge set by Professor Mark Brearley in his interview in chapter four, they show that urban thinking and architectural specificity can enable mixes of uses and co-location in close proximity. The planning regulations in many countries need to move on from the two dimensional zoning practices born of the Industrial Revolution. Our housing solution could yet be one that recognises the particularities of our cities and embraces it as a place of complexity and difference.

At the heart of this book is a set of projects from which architects and housing managers all over Europe can learn. It offers a set of design strategies and technical criteria for doing things differently and optimising outcomes. But the built fabric of our cities is more than a series of commodities. When we design houses and housing estates we are designing new pieces of our cities, and thus creating the settings for our collective and personal experiences, places where we will work and play, places that will support our right to the city and our participation in all its nuances and multiplicity.

The way forward for public housing lies in good design enabled by people with a broad and sincere understanding of the issues, both cultural and social, economic and political. This book demonstrates that architects can again reclaim their historic role and be part of the solution to housing shortage if they are prepared to challenge development status quos, to collaborate and to adopt a diversity of roles. The future for housing and the sustainable regeneration of our towns and cities requires not only architects, but community enablers, planners and urban designers to work together and think differently. ▬▬▬

Country profiles

Austria

KEY DATA

Population	8,390,000 (2010)
Total number of dwellings	4,441,000
Tenure	Social rent 20.1%, private rent 28.3%, owner occupier 51.6%
Number of dwellings per 1,000 inhabitants	555
Total housing completions in 2012/13	52,000
Total number of social rental dwellings	891,000
Social housing production 2012/13	15,000
Providers	Municipalities, limited-profit sector (including co-operatives and companies), also limited provision by for-profit providers
Sources	2011 Census, GBV, Statistics Austria, Social Housing in Europe LSE, State of Housing in EU 2015, Housing Europe

Belgium

KEY DATA

Population	10,951,665 (2011)
Total number of dwellings	5,203,400
Tenure	Social rent 6.5%, private rent 27.5%, owner occupier 64.8%, other 1.2%
Number of dwellings per 1,000 inhabitants	473
Total number of social rental dwellings	292,000
Social housing production in 2012	3,076
Sources	Census 2011, Housing Europe General Survey 2014, Social Housing in Europe LSE, State of Housing in EU 2015, Housing Europe

Denmark

Population	5,614,000 (2013)
Total number of dwellings	2,762,000
Tenure	Social rent 19%, private rent 30%, owner occupier 51%
Number of dwellings per 1,000 inhabitants	491
Total housing completions in 2012	13,851
Total number of social rental dwellings	553,600
Social housing production in 2012	1,250
Providers	Not-for-profit housing associations
Sources	Statistics Denmark, EMF Hypostat, BL, Social Housing in Europe LSE, State of Housing in EU 2015, Housing Europe

France

KEY DATA

Population	64,876,618 (2010)
Total number of dwellings	28,077,000
Tenure	Social rent 17.4%, private rent 21.9%, owner occupier 57.7%, other 3%
Number of dwellings per 1,000 inhabitants	423
Total housing completions in 2014	266,500
Providers	State, municipal, local authorities and housing associations
Sources	Social Housing in Europe LSE, State of Housing in EU 2015, Housing Europe

Germany

Population	81,800,000 (2011)
Total number of dwellings	40,545,000
Tenure	Social rent 4.2%, private rent 50.4%, owner occupier 45.4%
Number of dwellings per 1,000 inhabitants	506
Total housing completions in 2013	215,000
Total number of social rental dwellings	1,539,000
Social housing production in 2012	22,634
Providers	All market players - municipal or private housing companies, co-operatives or private investors - can access credit/subsidies to provide social housing
Sources	2011 Population and Housing Census, Destatis, Fachkommission Wohnungsbauförderung/SuBVE Bremen, Bundesbaublatt 6-2014, Social Housing in Europe LSE, State of Housing in EU 2015, Housing Europe

Netherlands

KEY DATA

Population	16,800,000 (2013)
Total number of dwellings	7,200,000
Tenure	Social rent 33%, private rent 7%, owner occupier 60%
Number of dwellings per 1,000 inhabitants	429
Housing completions in 2012	57,703
Total number of social rental dwellings	2,555,000
Social housing production in 2012	31,100
Providers	Housing corporations
Sources	Eurostat, Ministry BZK, AEDES, Google, Social Housing in Europe LSE, State of Housing in EU 2015, Housing Europe

Switzerland

KEY DATA

Population	7,639,961
Total number of dwellings	4,000,000
Tenure	Social rent 8%, private rent 54%, owner occupier 37.5%
Number of dwellings per 1,000 inhabitants	523
Total housing completions in 2013	46,000
Total number of social rental dwellings	300,000
Social housing production in 2012	n/a
Providers	Non-profit housing organisations and housing co-operatives
Sources	Swiss Federal Statistical Office, Eurostat, Co-operative Housing International

UK

KEY DATA

Population	62,698,362 (July 2011)
Total number of dwellings	27,767,000
Tenure	Social rent 18.2%, private rent 17.6%, owner occupier 64.2%
Number of dwellings per 1,000 inhabitants	437
Housing completions in 2015-16	134,940
Total number of social rental dwellings	4,936
Social housing production in 2015-16	30,440
Providers	Housing associations, local authorities
Sources	GOV.UK, DECLG, CSO Census 2011, Google, Social Housing in Europe LSE, State of Housing in EU 2015, Housing Europe

European housing timeline
1840s–2016

1849	First German housing foundation created in Leipzig by banker Christian Gottlobb Frege.
1860s	Philanthropists in Denmark help workers group together and buy land to build own developments and promote ownership as means to promote family/conservative values.
1862	Peabody trust established in the UK by George Peabody to provide affordable dwellings.
1862	First home-ownership housing co-operative in Germany founded in Hamburg.
1880s	Habitations à bon marché (HBMs), meaning inexpensive housing, is launched in France by privately financed philanthropic groups and industrial charities.
1885	The Housing of the Working Classes Act in UK empowers local authorities to undertake rehousing schemes by borrowing money against value of their local rates.
1884	Leipzig publisher, Herrmann Julius Meyer, establishes model tenements association for creation of affordable housing - by 1938 it is largest housing foundation in Germany.
1889	London county council established. It becomes one of the first and most prolific social housing builders.
1894	French Siegfried Act paves way for greater growth of lower-cost housing through state subsidies.
1902	Dutch Housing Act allows state loans to private companies and annual subsidies for affordable housing associations. Act also commits municipal authorities to creation of extension plans every 10 years.

1908	French Ribot Act introduces low-interest government loans to enable people to create housing for themselves through co-operative and mutual ventures.
1908	The Public Jubilee Fund established by Kaiser Franz Joseph becomes first public funding system of housing in Austria.
1910s	Danish movement of self-organised workers' co-operatives establishes cheap rental accommodation, becoming main basis of social housing across the country.
1919	Belgian Housing Law leads to creation of the Société Nationale des Habitations et Logements à Bon Marché (SNHLBM).
1919	Het Schip (The Ship) affordable housing scheme completed by Michel de Klerk in Spaarndammerbuurt, Amsterdam. Prime example of the Amsterdam School of Expressionist architecture.
1921	French Housing Act increases levels of subsidies available for affordable housing and a plan for 15 affordable garden cities is launched for the Paris region aimed at working classes. Similar schemes developed around Brussels in same year.
1927-30	Karl Marx Hof completed in Vienna. Designed by Karl Ehn for the city's socialist administration, it is a monumental scheme for workers and low-income families.
1933	Danish Housing Act enables first subsidies for non-profit housing associations.
1935	London suburb of Becontree completed and becomes largest council estate in the world.
1936	La Cité de la Muette housing scheme is completed in France, embracing modernist approach and signalling a shift in direction.

1946	Danish Housing Subsidy Act provides increased subsidies for housing co-operatives.
1947	UK Town and Country Planning Act revolutionises land purchase and scale of construction by local authorities.
1949	Brunfaut Act in Belgium promotes building of public housing.
1950	West German House Building Act - known as 'Ester Forderweg' (first promotion scheme) - state subsides available to house builders of all kinds.
1951	French 'Habitations à Loyer Modéré', or rent-controlled housing established.
1951	Danish Rent Act expanded and introduces regulatory control over entire housing stock.
1953	UK completes 220,000 council housing units in single year; becomes historic peak of state production.
1954	Austrian Subsidised Housing Act releases more subsidies for affordable housing.
1956	The UK Housing Subsidies Act offers local authorities more money for taller and denser developments.
1961	East Germany embarks on large-scale state housing programme with *Plattenbau* building systems.
1962	Urban planning law introduced in Belgium to curtail private housing sprawl.
1966	Work starts on the enormous Bijlmermeer modernist housing estate in Amsterdam.
1967	Parker Morris standards in UK introduces new housing regulatory guidance including minimum space requirements.

1968	Modernist Renaat Braem publishes Het lelijkste land ter wereld (The most ugly country in the world), advocating closer coordination of housing and spatial policy in Belgium.

1968	UK reaches historic peak total housebuilding with over 352,000 completions.

1968	Partial collapse of Ronan Point in Newham, London. Doubts raised over quality and longevity of contractor-led panel systems of construction.

1971	France reaches historic peak construction of affordable housing.

1972	Danish Planning Act prevents the sub-division of old properties into flats and selling them off individually.

1972	The city of Manchester completes the Hulme Crescents to become the largest new public housing development in Europe, with 3,284 deck-access homes for 13,000 people.

1975	Housing Agreement requires all private rented housing put up for sale to be offered to existing residents first - leads to boom in co-operative housing. Subsidies added as well.

1980	UK Conservative government introduces Right to Buy, offering council tenants the opportunity to buy their council house at a substantial discount.

1980	Social housing in Belgium is decentralised to three regions: the Flemish Region, the Walloon Region and the Brussels-Capital Region. Each region develops its own housing codes and policies.

1980s	Municipal housing associations in Holland privatised and transformed into housing associations.

1981	Under UK Right to Buy, 160,000 council houses sold, removing them from local authority control.

1986	Decline of German state involvement in housing co-operative development, with the withdrawal of financial support.

1989	Work completed on the massive Marzahn estate in Berlin, the largest socialist-led housing scheme in Germany.

1990s	Dutch social housing providers become independent of the state and are encouraged to be more entrepreneurial.

1993	Private guarantee fund in Holland sees state take up default risk to support ownership among lower-income group.

1995	Dutch Grossing and Balancing Operation act withdraws state subsides to housing associations and encourages them to be financially independent.

1995	Riots in the banlieue of Paris highlight tensions between the city's prosperous heart and vast network of outlying system-built estates.

1997	New Labour comes to power in UK. Prime Minister Tony Blair shortly after appears on the raised walkways of London's Aylesbury estate with a promise to lift people out of poverty.

1997	UK Labour government oversees accelerated rate of housing stock transfers from local authorities to housing associations.

1998	French law passed stipulating a 20% affordable housing target for every town.

1999	Towards an Urban Renaissance is published by the UK government's Urban Task Force, led by Richard Rogers.

2000	British planning policy enshrines preference for brownfield sites for housebuilding.

2001	Danish Ministry of Housing and Urban Affairs abolished. Subsidies for housing reduced, but rent controls untouched.
2002	UK Housing Market Renewal Initiative - also known as Pathfinder - launched in northern cities. It leads to widespread demolition of old council housing and Victorian terraced properties. Few projects succeed due to economic reasons.
2002-03	Local authorities across the UK record just 180 housing completions - a record low for the post-war years.
2002-03	Completions by all UK housing associations plummet to 19,080 - half what they were just 10 years earlier.
2003	Swiss Federal Housing Act reconfirms housing as a basic right and legislation supports co-operative housing. Deals with the financial development means available to the non-profit sector.
2004	Last wholly municipal housing scheme built in Austria. The emphasis is put into public/private, municipal/housing association partnerships.
2006-07	UK housing legislation enables local authorities to build affordable homes on council-owned land and permits new borrowing within strict limits.
2007	Grenelle Environnement in France commits government to refurbishing 800,000 affordable units by 2020.
2007	Creation of greater municipal authorities in Denmark with more power over housing.
2007-10	Financial crisis reduces housebuilding and leads to reduced subsidies for councils and housing associations in countries across Europe.
2009	UK government announces plans for devolved local authority self-finance giving them greater freedom to borrow money for housing, but within strict caps. Becomes a reality in 2012.
2009	Austrian housing funding is devolved to the provinces.
2010	Belgian tax system changed to favour property ownership.
2016	New Housing Act in Holland requires 80% of annual new social rental units to be allocated to households with annual gross income of maximum of €35,000.
2016	The UK Housing and Planning Act enshrines policies to expand Right to Buy, abolish lifetime tenancies, introduce income-based council rents and a promise to build starter homes - effectively subsidising the private sector.

Glossary

Abercrombie Plan officially known as The Greater London Plan of 1944, it was developed by Sir Leslie Patrick Abercrombie (1879-1957) as a radical blueprint for the city's reorganisation. Its key recommendations included strict zoning of residential and industrial spaces, new housing, more open space, road building and reducing densities through decentralising the population.

Affordable housing any housing tenure whereby repayments are held below typical local market levels. "Affordable" is officially defined by UK government as 80% of market value, but housing associations and councils often offer it on a needs basis of between 50-60%.

Affordable rent defined by the UK Conservative government in 2015 as social rent tenancies charged at under and up to 80% of private market rents in any given area.

Alan Colquhoun (1921-2012) was a British born architect, historian, critic and teacher who started his career at the architects department of the London County Council and then working on housing with Lyons Israel Ellis.

Aneurin Bevan (1897-1960) was a Labour party politician who was the minister for health in the post-war Attlee government of 1945 to 1951. As minister, he spearheaded the establishment of the National Health Service and advocated housing reform.

Banlieue French, meaning suburbs, but often now associated more with large post-war estates and economic and social isolation.

Bauhaus art school and design movement in Germany active between 1919 and 1933 and led by Walter Gropius. It advocated a radical collaboration between arts, crafts, design, architecture and production.

Bedroom tax also known as under-occupancy charge or the spare room subsidy. It is the nickname given to changes to housing benefit entitlement that means a cut in housing benefit if you live in a housing association or council property that is deemed to have one or more spare bedrooms.

Behavioural insights team a social purpose company jointly owned by the UK government and Nesta (the innovation charity), it champions the application of behavioural sciences in policy development.

Capped rent system by which there is a maximum rent or percentage rent increase that a landlord can charge for a property. The "cap" may differ according to the defined metropolitan area and may apply to either or both local authority and private rental properties.

Co-housing residential projects realised by "intentional communities", created, funded and managed by their residents. While households are typically self-contained, personal and private homes, residents come together and share activities, spaces and management responsibilities.

Community Infrastructure Levy (CIL) a planning charge, introduced by the Planning Act 2008 as a tool for local authorities in England and Wales to help deliver infrastructure to support the development of their area. Development which creates net additional floor space of 100 sq m or more, or a new dwelling, is potentially liable for the levy.

Community land trust a form of community development group, typically owning land, set up and run by local people to develop and manage housing and other community assets, which are then held in long-term stewardship to maintain affordability.

Compulsory purchase order legal function in the UK that allows certain bodies – usually the state – which need to obtain land or property to do so without the consent of the owner or by force.

Crowdfunding the practice of funding a project or venture by raising many small amounts of money from a large number of people, typically via the internet and social media.

Cross-subsidisation the practice of charging market prices to one group of residents to subsidise lower prices for another group. In housing it means a developer (public or private) simultaneously developing market-cost housing in order to pay for affordable units.

Custom-build process by which an individual works with a "hands-on" developer in the design and construction of their home, tailoring requirements for the end user and taking on much of the logistical elements.

D

David Gray (1930-2014) British architect who worked for the office of Erno Goldfinger before joining Lyons Israel Ellis and then Middlesex county council with Neave Brown and Richard Rogers.

Design and build term describing a procurement route in which the main contractor is appointed to design, manage and construct the works, as opposed to a traditional contract where the client appoints consultants to design the development and then a contractor is appointed separately to construct the works. In the UK, many such contracts are now are now started at Stage 4A where design drawings and specification have been developed to a more sophisticated level.

Discounted rent similar to "intermediate" rent, whereby a 20% discount is offered on housing association properties where the tenant is saving to buy.

F

Fabric first an approach to building design that seeks to maximise the performance of the components and materials that make up the building fabric itself, before considering the use of mechanical or electrical building services systems.

G

Gentrification the process of renewal and rebuilding accompanying the influx of middle-class or affluent people into historically deteriorating areas that often results in the displacement of poorer residents.

GLA Architecture, Design and Urbanism Panel The GLA and Transport for London (TfL) established a procurement framework of suppliers in order to promote the highest quality architecture, public realm, urban regeneration and sustainable development in the capital and to deliver the aims of the London Plan and the mayor's transport strategy.

Great Estates collective name given to the historic landowners in London's West End who laid out the city and built speculative housing in the 17th and 18th centuries.

Greater London Authority (GLA) Top-level administrative body for London headed by elected mayor of London and overseen by Assembly. Established in 2000.

H

Habitation à bon marché (HBM) form
of state-subsidised, rent-controlled
housing in France developed between 1894
and 1949.

Habitation à loyer modéré (HLM)
Replacing HBM, the French system of
rent-controlled housing from 1949 to the
present day.

Homes for Londoners initiative set up
by London Mayor Sadiq Khan in 2016 to
fast-track the building of genuinely
affordable homes to rent and buy.

Housing need survey methodology by
which local authorities assess housing
conditions in their area and future need
by means of resident surveys.

Housing revenue account (HRA) system
operated by all local authorities of
recording all revenue expenditure and
income relating to the provision of
council dwellings and related services.

Housing supplementary planning guidance
also known as housing SPG it provides
more detail and information on aspects
of legislation first defined by a
greater regional or city-wide plan.

I

Intermediate rent schemes provided by
councils or housing associations under a
subsidised rent of between 60% to 80% of
the typical market price for that area.
It is charged for a fixed period of 3-5
years in order to encourage saving for
a mortgage.

J

James Gowan (1923-2015) British
architect who set up practice with James
Stirling and with whom he completed the
celebrated engineering building at the
University of Leicester in 1963. Gowan's
early career was at Stevenage new town
and at Lyons Israel Ellis.

James Stirling (1926-92) British
architect who, among critics and
architects alike, is generally
acknowledged to be one of the most
important and influential architects of
the second half of the 20th century.

John Miller (born 1930) British architect
and graduate of the Architectural
Association. Set up Colquhoun & Miller
with Alan Colquhoun in 1961 and in
partnership with him until 1988.
Established John Miller & Partners with
Su Rogers.

L

LCC London county council was the first
London-wide municipal authority and
operated from 1889 to 1965 assuming
responsibility for directing strategic
urban improvements, transport and
housing. Replaced by the Greater
London council.

London Housing Design Guide first
published in 2010, the guide is not
part of planning policy but is aimed at
complementing planning documents and
encouraging designers to aim for the
highest quality around issues such as
minimum space standards, climate change,
daylight and noise.

London Plan statutory spatial
development strategy for Greater
London written by the mayor of London
and intended to provide an integrated
economic, environmental, transport
and social framework for the city over
20-25 years.

M

Market sale housing sold or available to
buy at full market value.

O

OJEU process the Official Journal of the European Union, the process of public procurement and notification of government tender opportunities and awards. Typically this procurement process has a pre-qualification questionnaire followed by a more detailed invitation to tender design/methodology stage.

Outline Planning Application (OPA) an application for outline planning permission allows for a decision on the general principles of how a site can be developed before going into detail.

P

Parameter plans drawings and proposals that define the scope of a particular development, often produced as part of an outline planning application.

Parker Morris refers to Parker Morris standards, established in 1963 as minimum space standards and adopted in 1967 as the basis by which state housing was planned and built until its abolition in 1980.

Passivhaus refers to a rigorous, voluntary standard for energy efficiency in a building, in which thermal comfort can be achieved solely by post-heating or post-cooling the fresh air flow required for a good indoor air quality, without the need for additional recirculation of air.

Planning performance agreements a project management tool which the local planning authorities and applicants can use to agree timescales, actions, fees and resources for handling particular applications.

Priority employment areas areas defined by local spatial plans where there is a need or opportunity for job creation and economic activity.

PRS refers to the private rental sector or private landlordism where market rents are applicable.

R

Registered social landlord general term for not-for-profit housing providers approved and regulated by government through the Homes & Communities Agency - vast majority of which are housing associations.

Reserved matters approval where outline planning permission has been previously granted, without full details of design elements of the proposal. An application is then necessary to seek approval on these matters. These are applications for approval of the reserved matters.

Right to Buy established in 1980, this UK policy gives secure tenants of councils the legal right to buy the home they are living in at a large discount. Approximately 1.5 million homes in the UK have been sold in this way. The "right" was abolished by the Scottish government in 2016.

Ronan Point a 22-storey tower block in Newham, East London, which partly collapsed in 1968 after a gas explosion. The spectacular nature of the failure - caused by poor design and poor system-built construction - and the widespread press around it led to a complete loss of public confidence in high-rise residential buildings.

S

Section 106 agreement mechanism which makes a development proposal acceptable in planning terms that would not otherwise be acceptable. Planning obligations under section 106 of the Town and Country Planning Act 1990 typically cover developer contributions to local infrastructure improvements, eg public open space, affordable housing, education and highways.

Self-build process by which an individual
directly manages the design, planning
and construction of their own home.

Shared equity process where someone
buys a given equity share in a property
sometimes with the aid of a mortgage.
However, while the developer and/or
government own the remaining share you
do not pay rent on it.

Shared ownership a system by which
the occupier of a dwelling buys a
proportion of the property and pays rent
on the remainder, typically to a local
authority or housing association.

Small and medium enterprise businesses
and enterprises which employ fewer than
250 persons and which have an annual
turnover not exceeding 50 million euro
and/or an annual balance sheet total not
exceeding 43 million euro.

Social rent rented accommodation owned
by housing association or council with
payments held below local market levels.

Special purpose vehicle (SPV) is usually
a subsidiary company with an asset/
liability structure and legal status
that makes its obligations secure and
distinct from the parent company. SPVs
have been set up by local authorities
to define commercial partnerships and
private fundraising on specific areas
of land.

Starter homes a compact house or flat
specifically designed and built to meet
the requirements of young people buying
their first home, typically developed
on previously underused commercial or
industrial land.

Strategic housing land availability
assessment (SHLAA) is a key part of the
evidence that supports a new local plan.
Its purpose is to identify land and
buildings with potential for new housing
in any given area.

Sydney Cook (1910-79) Camden borough
architect from 1965-73 who brought
together and led a team of young
architects. In the eight years of his
tenure they together realised 47 social
housing projects.

T

Toxteth riots in 1981 were a series
of disturbances which resulted from
pre-existing social tensions between
the police force and the local black
community. The riots lasted nine days,
resulting in the arrest of 500 people
and tainting the reputation of the area
from that point onwards.

Transport for London strategic public
body responsible for the transport
system in Greater London with oversight
on all tube and bus services. Also has
major land holdings across the city.

V

Vers une architecture commonly known
as Towards a New Architecture, this is
a collection of essays written by Le
Corbusier (Charles-Edouard Jeanneret)
advocating for and exploring the concept
of modern architecture. First published
in 1923 and in English in 1927.

Viability a development can be said to
be viable if, after taking account of
all costs including central and local
government policy and regulatory costs,
and the cost and availability of finance,
the scheme provides a competitive return
- desired profit - to the developer.

Index

Page numbers in **bold** indicate glossary terms

Image credits

Adam Khan Architects p 54-57, p 142-145
allOver images/Alamy p 47 top
Anne Lacaton & Jean Philippe Vassal, Frederic Druot, Christophe Hutin. Photographer: Philippe Ruault p 48 (all)
Architectural Design p 7 centre
Architectural Press Archive/RIBA Collections p 3 bottom, p 21 top, p 47 centre top, p 113 top & centre top
Arqui9 Visualisation p 40
ASSEMBLE p 70-72
Avenier Cornejo Architectes & Chartier-Dalix Architectes p 99-100, p 101 left (top & bottom)

Ben Quinton p 71 bottom right
biq architecten p 58-59
biq architecten & Stefan Müller p 60-61
Bordeaux Council p 113 bottom

Christian Richters p 98 bottom
Collection Het Nieuwe Instituut/BERL, 189.34 p 113 centre bottom

Daniel Hopkinson/arcaidimages.com p 47 bottom
David Grandorge p 120 bottom right, p 121

Edmund V.Gillon, Collection of the Lower East Side Tenement Museum p 89 top
Einszueins Architektur p 74-75, p 77 top left

Finola Moore p 91
Frederic Druot, Anne Lacaton & Jean Philippe Vassal p 50-53

Hackney Borough Council p 3 top
Hawkins Brown p 30-33
Haworth Tompkins Architects p 34, p 35, p 37 centre & bottom
Hertha Hurnaus (photographer) p 76, p 77 top right & bottom

Jack Hobhouse p 64 top, p 65
Janet Hall/RIBA Collections p 89 bottom
Jim Stephenson p 13 top, p 15
John Maltby/RIBA Collections p 7 top, p 21 bottom
Julien Lanoo p 104 centre, p 109

Karakusevic Carson Architects p 23, p 26-29, p 47 centre bottom, p 95, p 122-125, p 133-137, p 146-149
Keith Allan Jaggers p 21 centre (top)

LAN p 106-108
Luc Boegly p 101 bottom right

Mae Architects p 62-63, p 64 centre
Mark Hadden p 3 (middle)
Mecanoo p 96-97, p 98 top & centre
Michael Feser p 83 top right
Mikhail Riches p 38-39
Mole Architects p 78-80